The Bible On
Love

The Bible

on

Love

by D. DEDEN

Translated by JOSEPH A. ROESSEN

ST. NORBERT ABBEY PRESS
De Pere, Wisconsin
U. S. A.
1966

Biblical quotations are from the Revised Standard Version of the Bible, copyrighted 1946 and 1952 by the Division of Christian Education, National Council of Churches, and used by permission.

231.6
D36 E

Nihil obstat:

Samuel D. Jadin, O. Praem.
Censor deputatus

Imprimatur: 163808

†Stanislaus V. Bona, D.D.
Bishop of Green Bay
July 2, 1966

The *Nihil obstat* and *Imprimatur* are a declaration that a book or pamphlet is considered free from doctrinal or moral error. It is not implied that those who have granted the *Nihil obstat* and *Imprimatur* agree with the contents, opinions or statements expressed.

© 1966 ST. NORBERT ABBEY PRESS

Originally published as
De Bijbel over de liefde
Roermond and Maaseik, J. J. Romen & Zonen, 1964

Library of Congress catalogue card number 66 - 22816

Printed in the United States of America
ST. NORBERT ABBEY PRESS
De Pere, Wisconsin

CONTENTS

INTRODUCTION

In our language no term is as hackneyed and has lost as much of its luster as the word "love." It is like an old coin whose inscription and value are almost unrecognizable through wear. It presents itself as parent-child love, marital love or being in love; it may refer to love of a friend, an animal and a plant, one's country, art, science, and so on indefinitely. It can indicate a profane pastime or even be offered as a commodity; but it can also be of a high order, demanding true respect and honest surrender of the lover.

One often hears that in essence Christianity is a religion of love. This is correct, if one really understands the love God has for us and expects from us. There is nothing for us to decide since God himself has revealed it to us. He did this in human language, in certain cultures, in fixed territories, at definite times. To study the biblical doctrine of love one must keep in mind the common parlance of the time and then establish its meaning. New Testament writers almost always express God's love for us and our love for him with the Greek terms **agapan** or **aǵapè**. One might ask why these particular words are used. There are several other terms available in the Greek of that time which are not employed.

Philein or **philia** is seldom used; **stergein** or **storgè**
erân or **erôs** never in the New Testament.

Fr. C. Spicq, O. P. has recently written an out-
standing book on this question (see bibliography). We
may content ourselves with the results of his inquiry.
Without discussing the long development which these
terms underwent, we will concentrate on the meaning they gradually came to have with the advent of
Christianity. Since this new religion expressed its
preference for **agapè** (Latin, **caritas**), we may conclude that the basic meaning of this term best lent
itself to the concept of divine love. The following
survey may further elucidate this.

Stergein is mere natural affection incited by instinct and habit. It is a "being attached to," springing
from the notion of solidarity. Within a certain group
(family, town, country) there is an inborn sympathy
and interest of members for one another. Thus
storgè lacks the freedom of choice implied in **philia**
and the reverence of **agapè** and the passion of **erôs**.
A psychological or social bond is a natural motive for
the regard one has for another. In such a context
it is understandable that the New Testament did not
choose **stergein,** either to express God's free love
for man, or the religious love of man toward God
and neighbor.

Erân — erôs is still less proper for a purely spiritual
love since this term implies blind passion and
sensuous, often sexual, desire. This unreasonable
attachment for someone or something does not seek

the happiness of another, but selfishly hopes to conquer and enjoy. Erôs is therefore essentially always a self-seeking love.

Philein is love among friends. This is not blind, but free in its choice. Good in another arouses admiration and affection which also entails benevolence. Then reciprocated friendship develops along with mutual sympathy, trust and generosity — in a word, familiarity. According to the Greeks it was not possible to love a god in this way since friendship is mutual and therefore can exist only among equals. In short, **philia,** in spite of certain nuances, could have been Christianized since it offers a double advantage: it is based on nobility of character and does not connote the sensual. That it was not accepted in biblical terminology may be due to the fact that its profane usage had become too strictly personal and thus too political. It could not properly designate a gift of God. Consequently Christian language needed a less tainted term.

That was found in **agapân,** a term which in the Greek world had run a full gamut of meanings (Homer: hospitable reception; Isocrates: pleasurably disposed; Aristotle: bestow motherly tenderness, forfeit one's own interest); the noun **agapè** (lasting benevolence) was however still unknown or — at least in a religious sense — unusual. The Latin rendering of the verb is **diligere,** from the noun **dilectio** or **caritas.** Why Christianity preferred this term may be readily explained. The essence of **agapè** is in benevolence, because it always regards the well-being of the loved

and rejoices in his welfare. It rests less on emotion
than on the will, because it emanates from esteem
and respect for the other. It is generous, because it
is not self-seeking; it is even prepared to sacrifice
self for the welfare of the beloved. Moreover, it
expresses itself in deeds. In a word: it is a generous,
active benevolence, originating from respect for the
other.

In the final analysis the New Testament preference
for **agapân** or **agapè** is due to the Septuagint, the
Greek translation of the Old Testament, which
strongly influenced the vocabulary of the New Testament. This authoritative version shows a definite
preference for these two words. It uses **philia** infre-
quently, **erôs** twice, and **storgè** never; **agapân** by
contrast appears 268 times, **agapè** twenty times and
agapèsis ten times. A primary reason is that this
word seemed elastic enough to render all the
nuances of "love" (Hebrew **âhab** and its derivations)
mentioned in the inspired texts. It is used to indicate
entirely different kinds of love: parental (Abraham
for Isaac), friendly (David and Jonathan), neighborly
(usually restricted to a compatriot) and sexual (Isaac
and Rebekah, Michal and David, bride and bridegroom of the Song of Solomon; also the passion of
Amnon for Tamar).

But besides this greater adaptability of **agapân,**
for which the profane Greek in many cases would
have used another term, there is a second reason
why Old Testament translators preferred this term.
It has certain connotations also found in New Testa-

ment usage. First there is a **preference** for the beloved, which leads to exclusiveness (jealousy! Song of Solomon 8:6). Jacob has two wives but his love is for one; he has twelve sons but one is his favorite (Gen. 29 and 37). God placed many nations in the world, but his love is for his chosen people. He concluded a covenant with them, which he faithfully keeps and strictly guards, for he is a jealous God (Ex. 20:2). Another characteristic is that it is **motivated:** it rests upon esteem and always respects the loved one. Hence religious love manifests moderation and is contrary to stimulated passion, inspired only by beauty or charm. That is why **agapè** could be, and was, applied to the adoring love of creature for his Creator, and loving God becomes synonymous with fearing or adoring him. This expression implies two other traits, **mutuality** and **faithfulness** (both inseparable from the covenant idea). Hence God's commandment: "You shall love the Lord your God with all your heart, and with all your soul, and with all your might" (Deut. 6:5). From its context, this formula can only mean an exclusive predilection but it must necessarily be understood as contingent with a declaration of love for Yahweh and therefore as a human response and expression of gratitude; this is a religious and total love, dominating man's entire moral life. Israel must form its grateful love-in-return by adoring its divine benefactor and by obediently serving him. Love of God implies keeping his commandments. One feels how near we come here to "remain in my love" — of John. This is the true ethics of love, unheard of in the history of many pseudo-religions; in it moral life is conceived of as an unfolding of one's love for God.

The Greek Old Testament bridged the gap between a profane idiom and the New Testament, insofar as the latter borrowed its terminology for religious love from the common usage of the Greeks. This was enriched by the data of revelation concerning God's goodness to man and his total demands on him. We shall now see how this revelatory process developed.

I

GOD'S INITIATIVE

"I have loved you with an everlasting love" (Jer. 31:3)

One who inquires into the role love has played in the religion of Israel, soon perceives that the Bible speaks more of the love of God for man than of the love of man for God. If, in addition, he is mindful that this divine love is the reason for the existence of man's love-in-return, his attention will naturally focus on it. The incarnation conferred a new luster on divine love; this makes it advisable to treat the Old and New Testament separately.

A.

GOD'S LOVE IN THE OLD TESTAMENT

Old Testament religion centers around two points which, although paradoxical, clearly interpenetrate in traditional preaching. The one presents an infinitely holy God, inaccessible to sinful man; the other shows this same God entering into direct communion with man and becoming remarkably intimate with him.

One can compare the exalted majesty of God in the creation story with the fatherly God of the paradise narrative, both told in the opening chapters of the Old Testament, the one following the other without any distinguishing transition. In the paradise context — in his turning toward man — love, mercy, grace and forgiveness are essential. One searches in vain here for a systematic exposition of God's caring love, although this is everywhere undeniably present; as a constantly propelling force it can be detected throughout the Old Testament, at one time latently, at another openly as in Hosea, Jeremiah and in Deuteronomy, three related books which will receive special attention later.

God's love manifests certain facets in the Old Testament: it is community directed, reveals itself in salvific deeds, is totally unmerited and culminates in his mercy.

1. That Yahweh's love directs itself **to a community** immediately brings to mind the covenant idea. He made his pacts with a people and not with particular persons. His love for the individual is seldom mentioned. We hear of this three times and in each case a king is involved (in 2 Sam. 12:24 and Neh. 13:26 it is Solomon; in Is. 48:18 it is Cyrus). These texts may be influenced by the theory of divine sonship of kings, which could have penetrated into Israel under pagan influence. However, apparently no reference speaks explicitly of Yahweh's love for particular persons. This is proof that God's love is always regarded as collective.

2. This love of God for his people reveals itself in **salvific deeds.** It is more than a passing inclination. "I have loved you with an everlasting love" (Deut. 10:15; Jer. 31:3). It renews itself from generation to generation, follows its own plan, has its own aim. In a word, it is an active love.

It is well-known that Israel's faith was founded on religious experience of God. It had come to know him not in abstractions, not academically, but in the school of life, as his people repeatedly encountered him in the crucial stages of their national history when he delivered them again and again. It was he who chose Abraham and his generation. He guided and guarded them on their wanderings and brought them to Egypt. He protected them against the enticements of the cult of Baal in Canaan. When they became' slaves in Egypt, he again liberated them. He was their guide through the desert, cared for them, performed miracles for them. On Sinai he showed them the highest expression of his love by concluding a covenant with them and assuring them that he was to be their God, they were to be his people. He brought them to the promised land and helped them conquer it. He gave them Judges to protect them against their enemies, especially the Philistines. He came to live among them as their helper and refuge in the Jerusalem sanctuary; he gave them kings and prophets to guide them in politics and religion. He sent them into exile to cleanse them, and led them back as a small, selected people who began to prepare themselves for the

coming messianic salvific era. All these expressions
of his power were signs of his love for his people.

3.   These deeds of power were even more incom-
prehensible, insofar as they were absolutely **unmerited.** This leads us to election, the central idea of
the Old Testament which is best described in Deuteronomy. "Behold, to the Lord your God belong
heaven and the heaven of heavens, the earth with
all that is in it; yet the Lord set his heart in love
upon your fathers and chose their descendants after
them, you above all peoples, as at this day" (Deut.
10:14-15; Amos 3:6).

> "He found him in a desert land,
> and in the howling waste of the wilderness;
> he encircled him, he cared for him,
> he kept him as the apple of his eye;
> like an eagle that stirs up its nest,
> that flutters over its young,
> spreading out its wings, catching them,
> bearing them on its pinions"
> (Deut. 32:10-11; cf. 10:14).

The Deuteronomist asks what influenced Yahweh
in his choice. Certainly not their great number: "It
was not because you were more in number than any
other people that the Lord set his love upon you
and chose you, for you were the fewest of all peoples"
(Deut. 7:7). Nor was it their virtue: "Know therefore, that the Lord your God is not giving you this
good land to possess because of your righteousness"
(Deut. 9:6). The only motive for their election was

God's love (Deut. 4:37; 7:8; 10:15; 23:6, etc.). Ezekiel 16, in a crudely realistic allegory, expresses the same conclusion that this people by nature is not in the least attractive. He depicts Israel as a disowned maiden, lifted up by Yahweh, cared for and raised, and finally taken as his bride when she came of age. Yahweh chose this people he loved and saved of his own free will; nothing could have forced him.

Nevertheless, Israelite sensitivity constantly searches for a rational argument to justify its election. God, they say, loves his people and chooses them because of the covenant made with their fathers (Deut. 7:7 etc.; also Deut. 4:37 and 10:15), or because of his promise to David (2 Kings 19:34; Ezek. 37:35), or to glorify his name among the nations (Ps. 79:9; 106:8; Ezek. 41:21; Jer. 14:21), or to punish the nations (Deut. 9:4 etc.). Such motives often lead Israel to assume an attitude of superiority, diametrically opposed to the nature of God's love. The prophets constantly remind them that their election should be seen in its proper light and would be efficaciously understood only when God alone would be appreciated as the highest and final good (Deut. 6:5; 8:7-20) with all obligations and risks implied in this acceptance.

Israel's faith was truly tested in exile. Most Israelites thought that Yahweh had left his people to their own devices (Is. 40:27; 42:18; 49:14). It was the duty of the second Isaiah, the unknown poet of the exile to again convince them of their divine election. Their vocation is everlasting, as is clear

from his beautiful text: "But Zion said, The Lord has
forsaken me, my Lord has forgotten me. Can a
woman forget her sucking child, that she should
have no compassion on the son of her womb? Even
these may forget, yet I will not forget you" (Is.
49:14). Israel still remains the privileged servant of
Yahweh; the coming reinstatement will show this
more splendidly than the past.

4. A fourth characteristic of Yahweh's love, one
to which sensitive people are most susceptible, is
his **mercy**. Israelites associate mercy with tenderness
and loyalty. Tenderness (Hebrew: **rachamim**) is an
intimate attachment to another — a mother, a father,
a friend. Loyalty (Hebrew: **chesed**) gives it a solid
foundation; through it mercy is no longer a blind
instinct, but a justified and conscious goodness, based
on a sense of duty to remain true to oneself. This
conscious goodness includes the needy — widows,
orphans and penitent sinners.

It is remarkable that Old Testament Israel, after
having been chosen by Yahweh in Egypt, repeatedly
and constantly revolted against him. In spite of this,
it was never finally disowned, but forgiven many
times and continually restored to community with
God. It seems that this rebellious attitude toward
their faith is never a match for God's forgiveness;
it forms the core of Israel's belief and is unparalleled
in other religions. We hear of gods who show anger
with their people, as those of Babylon did with their
flood, or as the stone of Mesja depicts Kamosj, who is
angry with Moab, or of gods who punish bad

rulers, as was believed in Mesopotamia. But that a God forgives a whole series of conscious and deliberate revolts is unheard of outside Israel. Hence Micah exclaims at the end of his prophecy: "Who is a God like thee, pardoning iniquity and passing over transgression, for the remnant of his inheritance? He does not retain his anger for ever, because he delights in steadfast love."

This mercy of Yahweh, ". . . a God merciful and gracious, slow to anger and abounding in steadfast love and faithfulness," according to Exodus 34:6 and throughout the whole of the Old Testament (see Nah. 1:3; Joel 2:13; Jon. 4:2; Neh. 9:17; Wis. 15:1; Ps. 86:15; 103:8; 145:8) can be better understood from Israel's concept of sin. Sin is entirely contrary to God. God is power and his entire activity is intended to impart power and life; sin on the contrary, as a harbinger of death creates a state of impotence. God makes contact by a covenant; sin severs this connection: "Your iniquities have made a separation between you and your God" (Is. 59:2).

Sin is a rejection of God and causes a breach, as the history of paradise well illustrates. To obtain forgiveness the sinner must first return to God in all humility, to be converted. All punishment Yahweh sends has one pedagogical purpose: to effect repentance of the transgressor. Therefore even these punishments are expressions of his love.

This is clearly stated by the prophet Hosea. He sees God as the lover **par excellence;** sin for him can

accordingly only be a rejection of God's love. This
sensitive prophet sees no other motive for Israel's
birth than God's goodness: "I took them up in my
arms . . . and I bent down to them and fed them"
(11:3-4). Hosea elsewhere uses a metaphor of Israel
as a bride, but here he depicts her as a helpless
child, thus making the gratuitousness of her adoption more striking. This goodness defines the
essence of God perfectly. "No! I will not execute
my fierce anger, I will not again destroy Ephraim:
for I am God and not man. The Holy One in your
midst, and I will not come to destroy" (11:9). The
expression: "I am God and not man" visibly places
divine love above human love. The former cannot
be circumscribed by threatening emotions or motives.
It is completely self-sufficient. Its virtue lies, not in
its weakness but in its demands. The Lord insists
on ". . . faithfulness, kindness and knowledge of God"
(4:1): religion therefore is a matter of conviction.
That Israel was unfaithful to its vocation, is due
to its material well-being (13:6). For this reason
Yahweh wants to lead them back to the desert,
there to speak to their hearts (2:16): "I will again
make you dwell in tents, as in the days of the
appointed feast" (12:10). What was once the place
of the first encounter and the first love (2:16; 13:5),
will again be a material purification (2:5). The
spiritual exodus begins and opens the gates of hope
for reborn Israel (2:17); figures of paradisic prosperity
complete the announcement of a religious restoration
(2:18-20, 23-25; 14:6-8). But the most remarkable
passage is certainly 2:21-22, where Yahweh announces

that he plans to celebrate anew the wedding feast
with Israel by imparting, as gifts, the covenant en-
dowments which Israel seemed unable to preserve:
justification, commitment, love and loyalty. This is
God's dowry for his bride and this new union will
last for ever, as the people of God will enter into a
dispensation of grace. Then Israel shall "know"
Yahweh. Thus Hosea is an introductory tract on
grace. Relations between the Lord and Israel, here
beautifully analyzed by a sensitive and psychological
man, can be seen as a prefiguration of the relationship between God and the soul. Jeremiah 31:31-34
deserves consideration as a connecting link between
Hosea and the New Testament. Both prophets
contributed to a deepening of theology, with what
is equivalent to a real discovery of God. Neither of
them systematizes: for these great intuitive men,
personal experiences and the shock of the providential
events were occasions for deeper insights into God's
salvific plan.

Jeremiah's idea of God is similar to that of Hosea.
God is the bridegroom of an unfaithful people, whom
he loves with an infinite love (31:3) and constantly
invites to return to its original fidelity; grace enjoys
precedence over justice. God's love is unmerited but
enduring (21:4-5). He is the tender-hearted father
of his "dear son Ephraim" (31:20; cf. 3:19); the
people is his "darling child" (11:15; 12:7). His merciful love penetrates beyond the more juridical alliance
which existed of old between him and his people.

The ideal attitude of group and individual toward

God, as Jeremiah sees it now and hopes will obtain in the future, is in harmony with this. At the most tragic moment of his life (chap. 30-33) he prophesies the restoration of Palestine with Jerusalem as its religious center and a king from the house of David. The Old Covenant which has been broken will be replaced by a New. As indicated, the main passage here is 31:31-34. The new pact which God will make with Israel "after these days," possesses a spiritual and intrinsic character, whereby in reality it ceases to be the Covenant. In the future Yahweh shall directly influence the heart of man (31:33), he shall give him a heart (24:7); the law shall no longer be written on stone tables but upon the heart, so that there will be no need to teach it (31:32-34). All shall know the Lord (31:34). In spite of the traditional covenant terminology (31:33), this pact no longer has a national tenor, but is based on man's personal relationship to God, and can therefore be universal. It is no longer hedged in with contractual obligations, but in its content (know God), it is as unlimited as God's love from which it springs, and as the Christian agapè, for which it prepares. Jeremiah has not expressed the notion that religion is an interior affair so felicitously and so powerfully anywhere else. With this we are on the threshold of the New Testament, where Paul, John and Luke appear as heralds of God's mercy and love and of the human love which ought to make response to it.

Summary. The just and holy God, the inaccessible Lord of the Old Testament, cannot be seen in detachment from the God of a love preferentially given to his people Israel. Although several psalms mention his goodness to all creatures, this is called love only much later (Wis. 11:24). It is directed exclusively to Israel; it is the motive as well as the result of the election of this people, whom he leads out of Egypt to make the covenant on Sinai. This explains the nationalistic tendency of Old Testament piety: Israel's vocation is tantamount to its being placed above all other nations, a privilege made clear in the appellation "first-born son of the Lord" (Ex. 4:22). This fact also reveals how the God of the Old Testament is sovereign in his decrees, so that his love shows itself to be unmerited, emotional (it can change into anger) and paradoxical (love for an unfaithful people).

Deuteronomy especially presents the covenant as a revelation of God's electing and enduring love. The tone of this book is instructive and thus lacks the spontaneity and the more earthly style of the prophets. A number of them recorded the relationship between Yahweh and his people by using the marriage metaphor whereby one is reminded that the Lord's love was poured out on an unfaithful and disloyal people.

B.

GOD'S LOVE IN THE NEW TESTAMENT

1. Paul

Paul, called to be an apostle after the ascension of Our Lord, presumably had never known the earthly

Jesus. He did not concern himself with the earthly
career of the Master, which is the actual theme of
the gospels. His instruction was a doctrine of redemption, concentrating exclusively on the death and
resurrection of the Redeemer. He repeatedly returns
to this last and supreme moment of Jesus' life and
its meaning for us.

Besides this central one there is a second point.
Although we are redeemed in and through Christ,
Paul always refers all salvific initiative to the Father.
This theme also recurs in all his letters. He sees
our redemption as the intimate cooperation of Father
and Son, of him who planned it and he who carried
it out. An inquiry into divine love as presented by
Paul must look into the doctrine of redemption and
determine the roles played by Father and Son, and
their common motive.

a. **The love of the father.** That the plan of redemption emanates from the Father, can be determined from a whole series of related words referring
to God's will (Eph. 1:5, 9, 11; Gal. 1:4), his benevolence (Eph. 1:5, 9; Col. 1:19), his ordinance (Eph.
1:11; Rom. 8:28; 9:11; 2 Tim. 1:9), his decision (1 Cor.
4:5; Eph. 1:11). They are all so many aspects of God's
salvific will and have in common the fact that they
are all dictated by God's love. But his divine initiative goes further; his plan of redemption also entails
a number of preparatory acts: promise, election, pre-
destination and vocation. This is brought to light
in a wonderful way in two passages: Ephesians 1:3-14
and Romans 8:28-39, too long to quote here in their

entirety. These are the same acts which God applies
to Israel in Old Testament times. But the apostle
of the gentiles points out that they concern not only
Jews but gentiles too — in short, the entire divinely
predestined, chosen and called community of the
faithful. The introductions of his letters, addressing
the "elect" the "chosen" of the community in question,
especially indicate this divine initiative. This fact is
of great importance. It shows how the apostle follows Old Testament theology, which also refers all
salvation and justification to God. This divine initiative had a powerful apologetic value for Pauline
preaching which intended to eliminate or at least
reduce the scandal of the cross for his audience and
readers.

All these preparatory acts of God divulge his
infinite love; the quotations from Ephesians and
Romans, above, are actually poems dedicated to
God's love (Eph. 1:5 and Rom. 8:39 are especially to
the point). But this love has still greater extension.
It does not merely include the salvific plan and its
preparation; the execution itself emanated from God.
The Father sent his Son into the world of sinners
to save them (Gal. 4:4; Rom. 8:3; 2 Cor. 5:21); he
made him an expiation by his blood (Rom. 3:25) to
apply his saving justice to the faithful (v. 26); he
raised him from death (1 Thess. 1:10; Gal. 1:1; Phil.
2:9; 2 Cor. 4:14; Rom. 10:9) for our justification
(Rom. 4:25). Forgiveness of sin is his work, for
"God was in Christ reconciling the world to himself,
not counting their trespasses against them, and en-

trusting to us the message of reconciliation . . ." (2 Cor. 5:19). The substantial truth is that the whole work of redemption emanated from him. A special accent of love is given this divine salvific economy in a double formula: first, in the paradox that the Father redeemed us "while we were yet sinners (his enemies)" (Rom. 5:8), and in the touching words "God did not spare his own Son" (Rom. 8:32; cf. 2 Cor. 5:21); both of these converge harmoniously in Ephesians 2:4: "But God, who is rich in mercy, out of the great love with which he loved us, even when we were dead through our trespasses, made us alive together with Christ."

One thing is certainly made clear from all these saving acts of God: he is surely the God of love (2 Cor. 13:11), who loves his own (Rom. 1:7; 5:5; 8:39; 2 Cor. 13:13 . . .).

b.   The love of Christ. In spite of the strong conviction that all salvific initiative emanates from the Father, it is clear that Christ is the center of the work of redemption. God executed his plan only through him. One topic of special interest for us is Christ's relationship to us. Pauline theology is a doctrine of redemption, concentrating as it does on the death and resurrection of our Lord. It is also a fact that Paul naturally views his death as an expression of love.

A continuously recurring theme states that Christ "gave himself" for our sins (Gal. 1:4; 1 Tim. 2:6; Tit. 2:14). Paul explicitly declares three times that Christ did this out of love. In his letter to the Galatians, visibly moved, he exclaims: "I have been crucified with Christ; it is no longer I who live, but Christ who lives in me . . . the Son of God who loved me and gave himself for me" (Gal. 2:20). And to the Ephesians he writes: "Be kind to one another, tenderhearted . . . Walk in love, as Christ loved us and gave himself up for us, a fragrant offering and sacrifice to God" (Eph. 4:32-5:2), and a little further on he adds: "Christ loved the Church and gave himself up for her . . . No man ever hates his own flesh, but nourishes and cherishes it, as Christ does the Church, because we are members of his body" (Eph. 5:25-30).

The apostle therefore concludes that "Christ loves me," "Christ loves us," "Christ loves the Church"; on the strength of this love he gives himself for me, for us, for the Church. Three aspects of Jesus' love thus become visible: it is personal, collective and universal. Because of this threefold love he delivers himself to his executioners, as if to say: not Judas, nor the Jewish leaders nor Pilate have delivered me up, but my immense love; one here sees, latently, the logion of the synoptics: "For the Son of Man came not to be served but to serve, and to give his life as a ransom for many" (Mk. 10:45; Mt. 20:28).

We find a variant of this elsewhere: "If God is for us, who is against us? He who did not spare his own Son but gave him up for us all" (Rom. 8:31); this is obviously an allusion to the Greek translation of the fourth servant's song (Is. 53:6), which says that

Yahweh "laid on his Servant the iniquity of us all."
This reference, far from detracting from Jesus' love,
places it in its actual perspective; this is made amply
clear from the context, which represents the love of
the Son (8:35) as the manifestation of the love of the
Father (8:39).

The complete formula "He loved us and delivered
himself up for us" as mentioned (Gal. 2:20; Eph.
5:2, 25), can only mean that this love was the **cause**
of his sacrificing himself. The causality of his love
is not expressed more explicitly anywhere. There
are texts which combine this love and death, without
mentioning their mutual connection (Rom. 8:34-37;
2 Cor. 5:14), or they mention only his love (Eph.
3:19), or only his sacrifice for us (Gal. 1:4; 1 Tim.
2:6; Tit. 2:14); the "for us," accentuates the love of
Christ.

From this we may conclude that "delivering himself" and "giving himself" means more than just
"being crucified." The death on the cross as punishment for our sins would then have remained within
the sphere of justice. Juridically, the crime is expiated
independently of the attitude of the condemned;
with or without his consent, justice is done. God
could have been satisfied with such a business-like
expiation, or even with much less. But the apostle
does not concern himself with such speculations;
he sees only the fact that God clearly willed more:
that Christ gave himself up out of love.

How did the Savior make his love for the Father

and for men known? Paul replies: through his obedience and humility. In the first instance, he portrays this obedience by means of the Adam-Christ typology in Romans 5:14-21. The obedience of Christ cancels the disobedience of Adam. It is meaningful here that sin is referred to as "disobedience," redemption as "obedience." This is a true identification of the intrinsic act determining the morality of the subsequent execution. As Adam's trespass was disobedience of his will, so Christ's death was the expression of his submission. In the Christological hymn of Philippians 2:6 ff. his obedience and humility are even more broadly emphasized. The words "He humbled himself" and "He became obedient unto death" speak for themselves. The horrible position of a criminal's death on the infamous wood (verse 8: "to the death on the cross") makes the unique position of Jesus' sacrifice come through in still stronger light, insofar as it made him appear cursed by God in the eyes of his people (Gal. 3:13). The apostle expresses this altruism elsewhere in this way: "For you know the grace of our Lord Jesus Christ, that though he was rich, yet for your sake he became poor, so that by his poverty you might become rich" (2 Cor. 8:9). Against this background of extreme self-denial, one begins to feel to some extent what Paul really means with his elated cry: "He loved me and delivered himself up for me!"

The same unselfishness leads Jesus to share our misery in every respect except sin, so that we might better appreciate this in the future. "Therefore he had

to be made like his brethren in every respect, so that
he might become a merciful and faithful high priest
in the service of God, to make expiation for the sins
of the people" (Heb. 2:17). "For we have not a high
priest who is unable to symphathize with our weak-
nesses; but one who in every respect has been
tempted as we are, yet without sinning. Let us then
with confidence draw near to the throne of grace,
that we may receive mercy and find grace to help
in time of need" (Heb. 4:15-16).

The redemptive plan of the Father and the obedience of the Son spring ultimately from the same
source: their mutual love and their love for mankind. The first is the motive for the Son's obedience
to the Father in complete surrender; the second inspired the apostle with the terse formula of "God's
love in Christ Jesus" (Eph. 2:7; cf. Eph. 1:6; Rom.
8:39 . . .). In this case "in Christ" must not be
interpreted in an organic or local sense; it suggests
the solidarity between God's Son and humanity, on
the strength of which the whole of mankind is loved
in Christ by God. This dual love, God's and Christ's,
is expressed in the beautiful lesson read in the Mass
of the Sacred Heart: ". . . that Christ may dwell
in your hearts through faith; that you, being rooted
and grounded in love, may have power to compre-
hend with all the saints, what is the breadth and
length and height and depth and to know the love
of Christ which surpasses knowledge, that you may
be filled with all the fullness of God" (Eph. 3:17-19).
Although this text evidently refers to Christ's love,

the dimensions — breadth, length, height and depth
— indicate the same inexhaustible riches of the
salvific mystery mentioned in the preceding verses,
which occupy a central place in the letter to the
Ephesians. This saving work or plan of redemption
is precisely according to the initiative of the loving
Father. The closing lines of Romans 8 attest to the
same mutual love of Father and Son: "Who shall
separate us from **the love of Christ?** Shall tribulation
or distress or persecution, or famine, or nakedness,
or peril, or sword? . . . No, in all these things we are
more than conquerors through him who loved us.
For I am sure that neither death, nor life, nor
angels, nor principalities, nor things present, nor
things to come, nor powers, nor height, nor depth,
nor anything else in all creation, will be able to
separate us from **the love of God, in Christ Jesus,
our Lord**" (Rom. 8:35-39; cf. 2 Thess. 2:16 . . .).

John

While Paul concentrates so strongly upon cross
and paschal mystery, that he pays little attention to
Christ's earthly career, John considers the incarnation a mystery in itself. He also follows traditional
data, that the redemption was climaxed by the
death and resurrection of Christ; he even reserves a
special name for this decisive moment "the hour."
But for John, who, in contrast to Paul, was with
Jesus "from the beginning," the fact of Christ's
appearance in flesh took precedence as the day of
Jesus. This is the time of revelation, when it becomes clear that he is the Son sent by the Father,

who speaks his Father's words, performs his works and finally belongs in his Father's home. It is therefore true that John's doctrine of redemption points first of all to the incarnation of the Son. In his efforts to show that the absolute transcendency of the Son makes him preeminently suited to reveal the divine word, John seldom points to his human side. For him Jesus is not so much the prophet — as with the synoptics — as the divine wisdom, the Logos or divine organ of revelation.

In view of this central position of the Christ figure, it is worthy of note that John assigns a great role to the Father and even insists more strongly on love of the Father than of the Son.

a. The love of the Father. A first characteristic which draws our attention in John's theology, as in Paul, is that the initiative of the Father is brought so strongly to the fore. The Father sends his Son into this world (mentioned in John more than 50 times!), commits men to his charge (6:37-39; 17:6, 11,24), makes him do his works, speak his words (5:20; 12:49; 14:16, 31; 17:4, 8), lets him be a source of life for men (5:26 . . .). As he is a spirit, he seeks worshipers in spirit and truth and charges his Son with the instruction to institute a spiritual and interior religion (4:21, 24).

The entire salvific order emanates from the Father's love; his justice — again in contrast with Paul — is not mentioned. This love made him send his only Son: "For God so loved the world that he gave his only Son, that whoever believes in him should not perish, but have eternal life" (3:16). Contemplation of this inexpressible gift leads the apostle of love to his famous utterance, "God is love" (1 Jn. 4:8-16), the most exalted expression in New Testament revelation; the way for its final expression was already prepared by an older Christian tradition used by Paul (cf. Rom. 5:8 and 8:31-32; in 2 Cor. 13:11 one reads: "the God of love and peace will be with you"). The difference between the two is that Paul sees God's love demonstrated on Calvary, John places it in the incarnation.

The way John connects the idea of the salvific fact of the incarnation and the divine love is also significant for our subject. "God is love" means that he is love **for us.** We have no other criterion for measuring his infinite love than the gift he presented to the world in his Son. Hence the apostle does not deduce this love from a contemplation of God's nature but from experience; an unprecedented fact brings him to the statement: "God is love" (3:16; 4:9-10; 6:32-33). In this regard he follows completely the trend of Old Testament experience of God. He seems amazed that God who gives himself (in the incarnation, in the Eucharist) is the same God of the Old Testament, the God of the fathers.

Another remarkable characteristic is that John pays even more attention to the Father's love than to the Son's. "The Father loves the Son, and has given all things into his hand"; "For the Father loves the Son, and shows him all that he himself is doing"

(3:35; 5:20). In his high-priestly prayer Jesus says: "You have loved me before the foundation of the world" (17:24b). What the Son offers, in harmony with this Father-love is — in John as in Paul — his obedience. "For this reason the Father loves me, because I lay down my life, that I may take it again." Further, "If you keep my commandments, you will abide in my love, just as I have kept my Father's commandments and abide in his love" (10:17; 15:10). Especially through his obedience the Son reveals how much the Father loves us. He accepts his sufferings freely "So that the world may know that I love the Father, and I do as the Father has commanded me" (14:31).

The number of texts in the writings of John which mention Christ's love is disappointing. Only once do we hear of his love for the Father (14:31), and never of his love for mankind. His love seems to encompass only certain persons (11:5; 13:23; Rev. 3:9, 19) or the group of his disciples (Jn. 13:1). As regards his attitude toward his disciples, one learns incidentally that it is a reflection of the love of the Father for the Son (15:9; that it is a model for the love for one's neighbor which is the only way to remain in his love (14:21; 15:10) and that it was the motive of his redeeming death (15:13; 1 Jn. 3:16; Rev. 1:5). That is all.

Naturally these few texts are not sufficient to do justice to Christ's love in John. When one gives himself up with all he possesses for another, it is superfluous to express his love explicitly over and over again. So the love of Christ in the fourth gospel should be measured from what he actually brought us. The immeasurable riches he bestowed on us speak eloquently of his infinite love for us, without using the word.

What then are these incomparable riches for which his incarnation makes us thankful?

b. The benefits given by the Son. The introductory verses of the prologue imitate the creation narrative of Genesis (in the beginning — the word of God or God's speaking — all things were made — the light that shines in the darkness). This imitation is purposeful, presenting as it does the Godhead of the Son in sharp relief: "He was with God, and was God and all things were made through him." Further on John will assure that "No one has ever seen God; the only Son, who is in the bosom of the Father, he has made him known" (1:18). No one was therefore more qualified to act as organ of revelation than the Son, who is consubstantial with the Father and through whom the world was made (vv. 1-3). Starting with his incarnation, John sees him as the revelation of God to men, and designates him with the title, Word of God. According to the prologue this Word-made-man unites two functions: he is our **light** and our **life.** As we shall presently see, the theme of Christ as our light and our life sets the pattern for the entire fourth gospel.

1. The Prologue. "The Word was the light of men" (v. 4) means therefore that Christ was the

revelation of God. "And the light shines in the
darkness (sinful, unbelieving mankind) and the darkness has not overcome it" (v. 4). Obviously, the
revelation does not work automatically, but expects
recognition from man (v. 10), acceptance (11-12).
This human response is faith. At the end of his
gospel the apostle assures that his only purpose in
writing was to bring faith to his readers or to
strengthen it in them: "Now Jesus did many other
signs . . . that you may **believe** that Jesus is the
Christ, the Son of God, and that **believing** you may
have life in his name" (20:30). The same is found
in the prologue: "To all who believed in his name,
he gave power to become children of God" (1:12).
Faith enables revelation (the light) to change us into
children of God (the life); through it the work of
Christ becomes a new creation (as in Paul).

2. In the **gospel itself** the theme, Christ our light,
returns in different variations. Jesus can call himself a "witness" because he testifies to what he has
personally seen and heard from the Father (3:11-13,
31-33; 8:13-18, 28; Rev. 1:5; 3:14). His testimony
does not stand alone; it is confirmed by the Father,
Scripture, the Baptist and not the least by his own
words, all of which witness for him. After his de-
parture it is the Spirit who carries it on and deepens
it; assisted by the same Spirit, the disciples and the
Church continue to give testimony of him.

As a part of his revelation, Jesus shows his own
or his Father's "glory." John has a proclivity to date
Jesus' earthly career from the hour, the resurrection.

The result is a certain anticipation of his glory, just as his public life shows Jesus' glory, his Godhead. But it is a veiled revelation, known only to the faithful, and it is therefore no impediment that the actual glory of Jesus remains reserved for the future, as portrayed in the synoptics (12:28; 13:32; 17:15). The signs which he performs show Jesus to be the real messenger from God, he who came to bring the redemption foretold by the prophets.

This salvation is not only revealed but presented. John, convinced that the world is sinful and under the mastery of the devil, maintains the traditional view that salvation depends above all on Calvary and Easter (1:29; 10:15-18; 12:24). He characteristically gives the assurance that instruction by the present Son of God already liberates man. A text like 8:31, ("If you continue in my word, you are truly my disciples, and you will know the truth and the truth will make you free"; cf. 15:3) is significant in this respect.

3. The light and the life, because they are mentioned in the prologue, would seem to call for further development; they are subsequently symbolized as **water** (faith, baptism, purification) and **blood** (wine, explicitly mentioned at the wedding feast in Cana and presumed in chapter 6 as the Eucharist). Water and blood also flowed from Jesus' pierced side (chap. 19; cf. 1 Jn. 5:5).

The first half of the fourth gospel concentrates entirely upon these two symbols. (1) At the wedding

feast in Cana water and wine (blood) foreshadowed
the renewal; (2-3) in the case of Nicodemus and the
Samaritan woman, the light of faith, under the
symbol of water, is first presented to a Jew, then to
a non-Jew; (4) the healing in Capernaum: "Go, your
son will live"; (5) the lame man near the pool in
Bethzatha: the healing water, for which Jesus' word
supplies the desired effect; (6) the multiplication of
the bread: the life-giving bread from heaven is the
Eucharist, which implies the passion, the blood, the
wine; (7) the healing of the man born blind indicates
the culminating perfection of the light, while (8) the
resurrection of Lazarus does the same as regards
life. So we see that after the introductory miracle
of the changing of water into wine (the light of the
Old Testament makes room for the life of the Gospel),
there are the two great themes, which we have indicated by numbers: 2, 3, 5 and 7 point to the light;
4, 6, 8 to the life.

We have seen that the **light** (and its association
with revelation, testimony, signs) brings every one
who accepts it in faith the **life** (with its associations
of liberation, children of God etc.). Water and
blood act as symbols of the light and the life. Without any doubt, this symbolism points to the redeeming death, from which the gospel preaching draws
its saving power. The exactitude of this observation
is confirmed by Paul. He too, in his own way,
teaches that the light brings the life ("The gospel
is the power of God for salvation to every one who
has faith"; Rom. 1:16). He teaches that this is pos-

sible only by means of the preceding redemption,
("The word of the cross is . . . to us who are being
saved the power of God"; 1 Cor. 1:18; cf. Gal. 3:1
and 6:14). So the symbols of the blood and water
lead us inevitably to the "hour," the most sublime
revelation of the light and the actual source of our
life, the death of Christ on the cross, from whose
open side John saw blood and water flow.

3. Luke

Jesus' expiatory death for us on the cross was the
highest expression of his love (thus Paul and John);
the very first expression of his love was made in
the incarnation which brought us light and life (John).
Between this beginning and end lies his public life,
the time of mercy. John mentions his forgiveness of
the adulterous woman, but Luke, with good reason,
is especially known as the evangelist of the Savior's
mercy (cf. Lk. 7:36-50; 15:11-32; 18:10-14; 19:1-10;
23:34, 39-43). Jesus' self-revelation is touchingly
beautiful in Luke 15, which presents three parables
of lost things: a sheep, a coin and a son. The first
two follow an identical pattern: loss - search - recovery - joy - invitation to share in the joy. In the
third, the prodigal son, the search and recovery
(which therefore certainly cannot be essential are
missing, but the element of conversion is new and
the stronger stress on the joy (exhuberant welcome by
the father) is new. This is comparable to the happiness of the angels in heaven, mentioned in the two
previous parables, and to the understandable invitation to take part in the joy. The three parables have

one main common theme: joy over the recovery and the invitation of others to share in this happiness. These reach their greatest expression in the third parable. This is Jesus' answer to the pharisees who took his kindness toward sinners badly (cf. vv. 1-2). He is exceedingly pleased with the conversion of sinners vv. 7, 10, 20); the pharisees (the elder son) are irritated. In all three parables Jesus asks understanding for his forgiving love: the introductory verses show that "he receives sinners." In his human activities, he is God's mercy, seen and realized (cf. Jn. 14:9).

"Rejoice with me," is the glad message and motto of this chapter. It is a joy for Jesus to call sinners together and accept them: he had come to seek what was lost (cf. Lk. 19:1-10).

There is a threefold axis around which this chapter really turns: father - son - brother. This ideal relationship is projected against the background of another: slave - master. The younger son, ground down by the vicissitudes of life, realized what fatherly love meant to him, and this led him to repentance: "Father, I have sinned against heaven and before you; I am no longer worthy to be called your son." The real reason for the joyous celebration which followed is given in one succinct phrase: "This son of mine . . ." (v. 24). The elder brother however feels himself degraded: "These many years I have served you" (v. 29). He sees only commands and prohibitions, but no kindness. "I never disobeyed your command" and because of this he expects some reward ("at least a little goat") while this good-for-nothing "has devoured your living." He considers the feast a reward, while in actuality it was the inevitable gesture of an overjoyed father. Because he (and the pharisees exemplified in him) is unaware of what fatherly love is, he understands nothing of brotherly love either; not once does he call the other his brother. In a word, his role is that of a servant, not one of an actual child.

In Luke 15 one notes that Jesus joyfully receives sinners. Although there is no mention of expiatory death and vicarious suffering, this reception of sinners is nevertheless a redeeming love. Jesus is the one mediator in and through whom the heavenly joy of the Father is shown through the return of a sinner. His redeeming love is at the same time the creative love of God: "this son of mine was dead, and is alive" (v. 24) — he is again reinstated into his sonship. This act of pure goodness — "and he had compassion" (v. 20) — is applied to God in most translations. One may well ask whether this father, who is described as almost overcome with joy, felt only compassion and no stronger emotion. The Greek word **splangizomai** derives from **splangos**=the viscera, the bowels. We think we are true to the cultural imagery of that time, when we supplant it with our own cultural symbol of "heart," and translate: "his heart went out to him," or "his heart was touched."

The pharisees were coolly caluculating and assumed their usual juridical attitude. Jesus' love was for them a non-existent world; that was their heresy.

Their descendants exist today — people who do not want to know that over and above rigorous retribution there is always unmerited goodness, a very special kind of love!

Perhaps this is the place to say something about a totally different attitude of God toward men, namely his anger. If the divine mercy is so tangible, what is one to think of passages which speak of **God's anger?** Marcion — and after him many others — have seen a contrast between the God of the Old Testament and the God of the New Testament, as avenger and as a loving Father. This is definitely incorrect; both Testaments speak of God's love — as we have seen — and both speak of his anger, but on a different frequency.

God's anger in the New Testament differs in two ways from that manifested in the Old. In the Old Testament it is usually eschatological. It is the same in nine of the thirteen passages in which Paul speaks of God's anger. In the New Testament it is less personal than is his love; in other words, God's anger is the result of human sin, but his mercy is not the result of human goodness: this belongs to the nature of God himself. Consequently, God's anger is presented by the Baptist as impersonal ("You brood of vipers, who warned you to flee from the wrath to come?") and by Jesus himself ("For great distress shall be upon the earth and wrath upon this people" Lk. 21:23) and by Paul, who in thirteen passages describes anger only three times as being "from God." While he freely says that "God has loved us" (2 Thess.

2:16; Eph. 2:14) and that "we are beloved of God"
(1 Thess. 1:4; Col. 3:12), he never says that "God is
angry." Obviously, he thinks differently about God's
anger than about his love. He maintains the Old
Testament view of God's wrath, but uses it not so
much to describe God's personal attitude as the
inevitable process of cause and effect in the moral
order. "Wrath" depicts divine punishment in human
way, as this is implied in the moral order. Man
brings upon himself this punishment; sin is followed
by its inevitable result: "But by your hand and
impenitent heart you are storing up wrath for yourself on the day of wrath, when God's righteous
judgment will be revealed" (Rom. 2:5); but this
whole process is executed under God's plan, so that
Paul continues: "He will render to every man according to his works."

Conclusion: When the New Testament speaks in
a human way of God's wrath, this does not imply a
mood or disposition of God, but rather that sin brings
its own punishment. God does not reject the sinner
but the sinner rejects him. This is possible because
he has not placed us in a world in which his love
would mechanically protect us against the effects of
sin. "The wages of sin is death," even though "God
wants not the death of the sinner, but that he be
converted and live." Hence the inevitable choice for
man: either God's love through faith in his Son,
or God's wrath by rejecting that faith (Jn. 3:36).

Summary. The New Testament adds no new virtue
to God but the complete revelation of his love,

which he reserved for the end time. This consists of giving his Son for mankind. Though God's love is not mentioned as such in the synoptic gospels, it is made unmistakably clear in the activity of the beloved Son, who brings his immeasurable love for sinners in the word of forgiveness. In this manner his saving love is manifested in the person of Jesus Christ. This mercy is most strikingly depicted in the gospel of Luke.

The actual theologians of God's love however are Paul and John. Both agree in maintaining the Old Testament tradition that all salvation comes from God, source of all love; they also hold to the New Testament teaching that God has proved his love in sending us his Son (Rom. 5:8; Jn. 3:16) even though we were his enemies (Rom. 5:8; 1 Jn. 4:10). For both it is Jesus Christ who reveals and brings the love of God; his human contribution is his obedience. Finally, for both, the divine love operates in us to make us children of God and give us the ability to love one another. So far both sacred authors are broadly parallel. John emphasizes, more strongly than Paul, the love between Father and Son and that God's love for us is already realized in the incarnation. Paul on his part insists more on the love which manifests itself in the mystery of redemption, the sacrifice of the cross and the fact that we are crucified with him. The Spirit of the risen Christ to whom John reserves the fullness of the revelation, is in Paul the principle of interior enlightenment; nevertheless, above all, it is he who infuses God's love in us and makes it work in our hearts.

C.

SYMBOLISM OF LOVE
IN THE BIBLE

In the description of God's fatherly love for his people the Bible uses symbolism over and over again. With the love-symbolism of the Old Testament one must be careful of exaggeration. The comparisons (father-child, bridegroom-bride, etc.) should not be understood as in their modern, western meaning, but must be viewed from their accepted usage in ancient eastern culture; otherwise one runs the danger of producing a false picture.

The Old Testament was preparation for the New, and one must therefore leave room for expansion in the revelation itself. Our present knowledge of God's goodness and love cannot be presumed in the people of the Old Testament, who were still deprived of the light which Christ was to bring to the world. Ancient man was accustomed to picture heavenly events in earthly images, and saw his God above all as a king. As a child of its time and environment, ancient Israel did the same, especially since it was thankful for its existence as a nation to the Sinai covenant: "I will be your God and you my people." The **kingdom of God** (or, if you prefer, God's dominion) applies to both Old and New Covenant as regards the central content of the salvific message; the accents however — because of the Incarnation — are different. For the Israelites, full stress was put

on the royal attributes of Yahweh: his irresistible
power, inscrutable wisdom and strict justice. As a
result, devotion to him consisted mainly in reverence
and submission.

This theocratic attitude and creed created a sphere
of law (command - justice - submissiveness), wherein love could not as yet breathe. This was to endure
until the coming of the prophet Hosea, before any
one presumed to designate Yahweh's attitude toward
Israel as "love." Seen against this background, it
becomes clear that several images — king-people,
shepherd-flock, vinedresser-vineyard, etc. — refer pri-
marily to God's kingship; only the circumstances
and the context will prove whether or not this relationship can be termed a truly loving one.

The **symbol of shepherd** as applied to gods and
kings was already known to the Sumerians, the
Assyrians and Babylonians; for them the king was
regarded as one who cared for and led his subjects.
This symbol had real meaning for Israelites, former
nomads. Though Yahweh is seldom explicitly called
"shepherd" (two old references in Gen. 29:24; 48:15
and two invocations in Ps. 23:1; 80:2), he is however
equivalently depicted as such. He leads his flock,
going before them (Ps. 68:8), guides them to grassy
fields and water holes (Jer. 50:19), protects them with
his staff (Ps. 23:4), gathers them (Is. 56:8) and "gently
leads those that are with young" (Is. 40:11). These
expressions make it very clear that Israel is
cared for and led by Yahweh. Generally speaking
however, he entrusted the function of shepherd to

others. But these failed and were unfaithful. They did not seek Yahweh (Jer. 10:21), they resisted him (2:8) did not care for the flock (Jer. 23:1; 50:6; Ezek. 34:1-10) and looked after themselves (Ezek. 34:3). Yahweh himself had to gather and tend the scattered flock (Jer. 23:3; 31:10) and appoint better shepherds (Jer. 3:15; 23:4). He finally told them: "I will set up over them one shepherd, my servant David, he shall feed them and be their shepherd. And I, the Lord, will be their God, and my servant David shall be prime among them; I, the Lord have spoken" (Ezek. 34:23 ff.). Judah and Israel would be one people under one shepherd (37:22-24). Using this term, Ezekiel was to banish the idea of a purely political leader; he left the way this was to be accomplished to God.

Zechariah gives a final stroke to the messianic picture of the shepherd. After the return from exile there are still bad shepherds who rouse Yahweh's wrath (Zech. 10:3; 11:4-17). He summons the sword: "Awake, oh sword, against my shepherd, against the man who stands next to me . . . Strike the shepherd, that the sheep may be scattered" (Zech. 13:7). This divine judgment is the beginning of the purification, from which, as a remnant, the people of God of the coming time of salvation shall be brought forth (v. 8). The shepherd struck by the sword originally indicated the worthless shepherd of 11:15; in a present context however the text can only refer to "him whom they have pierced" (12:10) whose death heralds the salvific time (13:1-6). Thus

at the end of these Old Testament symbols we find
a foreshadowing of the shepherd who accepts death
according to God's will and thereby initiates the
final stage.

The prophecies are fulfilled in him who "gathers
the lost sheep of the house of Israel" (Mt. 15:24;
Lk. 19:9), the shepherd who shall die and rise again
(Mk. 14:27). It is he who says of himself, "I am the
good shepherd" and verifies this by his intimate
attitude to his followers, so that "I know mine and
mine know me" expresses not only a knowledge but
loving concern. This shepherd is prepared to give
his sheep life and plenty and even his own life (Jn.
10:14-15 and 10). His function as shepherd is universal; when he brings in "other sheep" also, the
promise of "one flock, one shepherd" will be fulfilled.
Christ is pictured as the ruler over Israel, promised
in Micah 5:3 (Mt. 2:6). In his earthly appearance he
is filled with compassion, and laments the flock
without shepherds (Mk. 6:34; Mt. 9:36); in his glorified
state he is the Lamb, who tends the countless numbers free from oppression and leads them to the
water holes of life (Rev. 7:17; cf. 14:4); on his return
he will be the apocalyptic ruler, who "shall tend with
an iron rod" the gentiles (Rev. 12:5; 19:15) and who
shall separate the sheep from the goats (Mt. 25:31).

In Palestine, the **vineyard** too demanded the
constant care and concern of the owner. The prophets frequently call Israel the vineyard of God.

"My beloved had a vineyard on a very fertile hill;
He digged it and cleared it of stones,

and planted it with choice vines;
he built a watchtower in the midst of it,
and hewed a winevat in it;
and he looked for it to yield grapes,
but it yielded wild grapes.
What more was there to do for my vineyard,
that I have not done in it?
When I looked for it to yield grapes.
why did it yield wild grapes?"   (Is. 5:1-4).

Yahweh brought a promising vine from Egypt to Palestine and there cared for it extremely well (Ps. 80: 9-12); its value of course depended on production, for of itself it was no more than firewood (Ezek. 5:1-9). For that reason it was planted in good soil (Ezek. 19:10; Is. 5:1) and shielded from everything harmful. Yahweh was faithful and devoted, but over and over again his love was confronted with a worthless vineyard (Jer. 2:21; Is. 5:1-5; 27:2-5). A better stock was needed, one God would plant himself in the new Israel — the Church (Mt. 21:28-46). The testimony of Christ: "I am the true vine and my Father is the vine-tender" evidently means the same thing. He is not a part of the people of God; he himself is that people. The reference here apparently presents a communal view of Christ: who remains in him, bears fruit; who does not, withers and is burned.

There is still another line of development which runs parallel with that of the worthless shepherd and the flock; it also leads to Christ. Jesus briefly sums up the history of Israel. God continuously waited for fruit from his vineyard; but instead of

listening to him the vine-tenders beat the servants
he sent (Mk. 12:1-5). In the excess of his love he
then sent his beloved Son (12:6); in reply, the
leaders of the people filled the measure of their
unfaithfulness by killing the Son, the heir of the vineyard. For that reason the guilty ones would be
punished, but the death of the Son introduced a new
stage of God's salvific plan: the vineyard was entrusted to faithful tenders, finally to bring forth
fruit (12:7 ff.).

As life and vitality are gifts of God, Yahweh is
the actual restorer, the only **physician.** Due to their
sins the people of God are ill and wounded and for
that there is no other medication than conversion.
God takes it upon himself to treat the patient in
danger of death with a painful but finally effective
remedy. In itself "physician" expresses not only love
and goodness but efficient help as well. There are
biblical texts in which the healing intervention of
Yahweh is prompted by love and he is pictured as a
loving physician. We find examples in Hosea and
Jeremiah, and in some of the Psalms.

> "When Ephraim saw his sickness and Judah his
>   wound,
> then Ephraim went to Assyria, and sent to the
>   great king.
> But he was not able to cure you or heal your
>   wound . . . .
> In their distress they seek me, saying,
> Come, let us return to the Lord,
> for he has torn, that he may heal us;

he has stricken, and he will bind us up.
After two days he will revive us;
On the third day he will raise us up,
that we may live before him   (Hos. 5:13; 6:2).

"I will heal their faithlessness;
I will love them freely"
(Hos. 14:4; cf. Jer. 13:12; 33:6).

As **host** Yahweh feeds his people with bread
from heaven (Ex. 16:4, 15, 32), at the same time a
benefit and a lesson for them (Deut. 8:2-5, 15; 29:4).
The messianic gifts are presented as a banquet to
which every one who listens to God's words is invited
(Is. 55:1-3). It is prepared for the whole world (Is.
25:6) as a spiritual banquet (Is. 2:2-4). Not content
with being host only, Yahweh will also be guest
among his people, first in the tent of the covenant
(Ex. 25:8; 29:43-46), later in the temple of Jerusalem
(1 Kings 6:13; 8:12). After the exile the people long
for Yahweh's return, and make it possible by recon-
structing the temple (Zech. 2:14). The devout wor-
shiper considers himself privileged to be allowed to
dwell with Yahweh (Ps. 23:5 ff.; 26:8 ff.). What then
must be said of that other Bread from heaven, with
which Christ nourishes his guests? Could there con-
ceivably be a more touching sign of love, than that
one gives his own body as food? Nothing less than
Jesus' own body feeds all guests unto eternal life; his
blood flows through their veins. What a most intimate union with the God-made-man, and what a
sublime brotherly bond among the guests (1 Cor.
10:16-18)! In and through our elder brother Jesus

Christ we have really become children of God and
may call this God "our Father" in heaven (1 Jn. 3:1).

This brings us to the **fatherhood** of God. Israel
considered Yahweh as its father, especially because
of its election and the covenant. Initially the chosen
people must have understood this in terms of a
powerful protection, with which he surrounded them,
as is obvious from Exodus 4:22: "And you shall say
to Pharaoh: Thus says the Lord, Israel is my first-
born son!" Only later (especially through Hosea and
Jeremiah) did they become aware that this fatherly
protector was guided by an immeasurable love:

"When Israel was a child, I loved him,
and out of Egypt I called my son" (Hos. 11:1).

"I thought
how I would set you among my sons,
and give you a pleasant land:
a heritage most beauteous of all nations!
And I thought you would call me, My Father,
and would not turn from following me" (Jer. 3:19).

"Is Ephraim my dear son?
Is he my darling child?
For as often as I speak against him,
I do remember him still.
Therefore my heart yearns for him;
I will surely have mercy on him, says the Lord"
(Jer. 31:20).

A culprit, condemned by any judge, may hope
for forgiveness from his own father; every child,

precisely because it is his child, may assert a right
to mercy which would be refused to a stranger:

"The Lord is merciful and gracious,
    slow to anger and abounding in steadfast love.
He will not always chide,
    nor will he keep his anger for ever.
He does not deal with us according to our sins
    nor requite us according to our iniquities.
For as the heavens are high above the earth,
    so great is his steadfast love towards those who
        fear him;
as far as the east is from the west,
So far does he remove our transgressions from us.
As a father pities his children,
    so the Lord pities those who fear him.
For he knows our frame; he remembers that we
        are dust"   (Ps. 103:8-14).

In the older books the Israelite did not call God
his "father" from personal devotion, even in the
psaltery. When the name does occasionally occur,
it is used by Yahweh himself and designates the
fatherhood of the entire nation. The reverential
fear thus engendered is also mentioned in the non-
biblical literature of Palestinian Judaism. It is only
in the hellenistic phase that one or other sage
(Sir. 23:1, 4; Wis. 2:3-18; 14:3) dares to pray to God
as his father. This establishes a bridge to the New
Testament.

A different line is introduced along with the
Israelite kingship. Since the time of David, the
fatherhood of Yahweh was especially connected with

a king (2 Sam. 7:14; Ps. 2:7; 89:27) as the legal repre-
sentative of the whole nation. Every ruler in the
Near East was considered as an adopted child of his
god; in the statement "You are my son" used in
Psalm 2:7; we find a Babylonian adoption formula.
Such texts about the sonship of the king prepare
way for revelation of the unique sonship of Jesus,
insofar as the real Messiah is already prefigured in
the kings of Judah. Another indication of Jesus'
sonship presents itself after the exile, when personified wisdom is introduced as the pre-earthly daughter
of God (Prov. 8).

In the New Testament God is addressed three
times as "Father": once by Jesus (Mk. 14:36) and
twice by the Christian community (Gal. 4:6; Rom.
8:15). The first time occurs in the Garden of Olives,
when Jesus prays, "**Abba,** Father!" The Aramaic word
abba expresses the familiarity of a child addressing
its father. To speak in this way to God was unheard
of in Old Testament Judaism. The Jews, who out of
reverence avoid addressing God directly, would
surely never have dared use such a familiar title.
The name reveals a very authentic trait in the prayer
of Jesus. From the hymn of joy (Mt. 10:32) it is
evident why Jesus could and would pray like that.
The logion makes it clear that no one ever addressed
the Father in this manner as did his own Son.

Paul testifies that the intimate title **abba** has justly
been passed on to us Christians. According to him,
God has redeemed us from slavery and adopted us

as his children (Gal. 4:5 ff.; Rom. 8:14-17; Eph. 1:5) through the faith of our baptism, which makes us one with Christ (Gal. 3:26 ff.); Christ as our eldest brother, who shares in the inheritance with his brothers (Rom. 8:17, 29; Col. 1:18). The Spirit, who effects this adoption from within, also gives testimony of it. He whispers in us the prayer of Christ himself, to whom he makes us equal: **"Abba**, Father" (Gal. 4:6; Rom. 8:14). In praying the "Our Father" the Church confesses her conviction that she is cherished with the same love, with which the Father loves the Son (cf. 1 Jn. 3:1).

One of the happiest expressions for God's love for men is implied in the name **bridegroom**. Israel is the beloved of Yahweh. He loves her with the same love a man has for his wife. Granted, this in only a symbol — actually, God loves his creature infinitely more — but as applied to the relationship of the Lord with man, it is a symbol enriched with all the nuances of intimacy, great tenderness, union, mutual surrender and fidelity, which mark married love. No other semitic people used this comparison to express the love between God and his people. In sacred history, the prophet Hosea was the first who dared parallel the Yahweh-Israel relationship with marriage. Apparently this was suggested — under light from above — by the tragedy of his own marriage. Introducing the Sinai Covenant as a marriage, he enriches it with an affective element through which it is idealized into a loving union of Yahweh and his people.

"I will betroth you to me for ever;
I will betroth you to me in righteousness and
    justice,
in steadfast love, and in mercy;
I shall betroth you to me in faithfulness"

(Hos. 2:19-20).

In reality however the love was one-sided. While
Yahweh eternally remained the dedicated and faithful bridegroom, Israel developed habits of infidelity
and adultery. No one in love is really jealous; therefore Yahweh reproaches his beloved constantly for
deserting and betraying him. We gather from this,
how the marriage symbol serves especially to determine the nature and gravity of the covenant infringe-
ments. In contrast to Yahweh's demand for worship
and true surrender, Israel flaunts its profligacy. This
infidelity, often compared with adultery, is a dis-
illusionment to the divine lover; it is a rejection of
his love.

Hosea made history with this comparison; it was
taken up by Jeremiah (2:2; 3:1-11), Ezekiel (16 and
23) and the second Isaiah (50:1; 54:5-7; 62:4-5).
Ezekiel stresses the generosity of Yahweh in polarity
with the ingratitude of Israel. "I anointed you with
oil. I clothed you also with embroidered cloth and
shod you with leather. I swathed you in fine linen
and covered you with silk. And I decked you with
ornaments, and put bracelets on your arms, and a
chain on your neck. And I put a ring on your nose
and earrings in your ears, and a beautiful crown upon
your head. Thus you were decked with gold and

silver; and your raiment was of fine linen, and silk, and embroidered cloth; you ate fine flour and honey and oil. You grew exceedingly beautiful and came to regal estate, and your renown went forth among the nations because of your beauty, for it was perfect through the splendor which I had bestowed upon you, says the Lord God" (Ezek. 16:9-14). And what was the reaction of the people on which God had lavished his benefits? The prophet describes it: "But you trusted in your beauty, and played the harlot because of your renown, and lavished your harlotries upon any passer-by . . . You also took your jewels of my gold and of my silver, which I had given you and made for yourself images of men, and with them played the harlot" (16:15 ff.). With sadness Yahweh recalls the happy time of betrothal.

"I remember the devotion of your youth,
Your love as a bride,
How you followed me in the wilderness" (Jer. 2:2).

This must be restored in the future:
"You shall be called My delight is in her,
and your land Married . . .
as the bridegroom rejoices over the bride,
so shall your God rejoice over you"
(Is. 62:4; etc.).

Yahweh will enter into a new covenant with Israel; the people's sorrow for the past will be a firm guarantee for their more solid fidelity in the future.

". . . I will allure her,
and bring her into the wilderness
and speak tenderly to her.

There she shall answer as in the days of her youth
. . . you will call me, 'My husband'
. . . and I will say: 'You are my people'"

(Hos. 2:14-23).

The prophets never tire of picturing the patience
and mercy of God's conjugal love. They admire his
strong will for union which remains steadfast despite
the defection of his beloved. Isaiah expressed this
emotionally:

"Your Maker is your husband,
The Lord of hosts is his name;
For the Lord Yahweh has called you
like a wife forsaken and grieved in spirit,
like a wife of youth when she is cast off, says
    your God.
For a brief moment I forsook you,
but with great compassion I will gather you.
In overflowing wrath for a moment
I hid my face from you,
but with everlasting love I will have compassion
    on you,
says the Lord, your Redeemer . . . . .
so I have sworn that I will not be angry with you
and will not rebuke you.
For the mountains may depart
and the hills be removed,
but my steadfast love shall not depart from you . . .
says the Lord, who has compassion on you"

(Is. 54:5-10).

There is still a question: Is this prophetic perspective found in the Song of Solomon, or is this book only a collection of love songs? Whether it is an allegorical portrayal of Israel's history or a song about married fidelity which the prophets in their turn utilized as a symbol of the covenant, the Song of Solomon still does not supply the key for this symbolism; it never identifies Yahweh as the bridegroom.

However tempting the allegorical explanation may be, it demands so much ingenuity that it seems better to regard this Song as a parable. It depicts a love, strong as death, whose inextinguishable flame is a symbol of the God's jealous love for his people (Song 8:6 ff.; cf. Deut. 4:24).

In the New Testament Paul applies this prophetic symbol to Christ and the Church. He could do this with reason, since the Baptist, "the friend of the bridegroom" had already referred to Jesus as "the bridegroom" and the Savior himself had compared the Kingdom of God to a wedding feast (Jn. 3:29; Mt. 22:2). The apostle graphically pictures the Christ-Church relationship in Ephesians 5:25-27: "Husbands, love your wives, as Christ loved the Church and gave himself up for her, that he might sanctify her, having cleansed her by the washing of water with the word, that he might present the Church to himself in splendor, without spot or wrinkle, that she might be holy and without blemish." How Christ's love towers above human love! This was unmerited: Christ did not love the Church because she was beautiful; on the contrary, he made her beautiful so that he could love her. This was

an unselfish love, which drove him to his death for
her. This was a noble love, which made him seek
the highest happiness for his beloved: "He gave
himself up for her, that he might sanctify her." A
man is not always able to give his wife beauty which
nature withheld from her; Christ could. No spot may
deface his bride, no wrinkle which might suggest
tiredness or old age (cf. Rev. 21:2, 9 ff.).

But this is not the final word! The most unselfish
and at the same time most indispensable kind of
love we can experience in our human life, has not
yet been mentioned: **mother love!** God also offers us
this most noble, most sublime and most tender love.

> "It was I who taught Ephraim to walk,
> I took them up in my arms;
> but they did not know that I healed them.
> I led them with cords of compassion,
> with the bands of love,
> And I became to them as one who eases the
>   yoke on their jaw,
> and I bent down to them and fed them"
>
>   (Hos.11:3-4).

From life's dawn to its twilight, from infancy to
senility, man is supported, carried and guarded by
God, as a babe in its mother's arms is cherished with
her love:

> "Zion said: The Lord has forsaken me,
> my Lord has forgotten me.
> Can a woman forget her sucking child,

that she should have no compassion on the son
of her womb?

Even these may forget,
yet I will not forget you" (Is. 49:14-15).

God's "mother love" is a lasting gift, a consolation
and a delight.

"Behold, I will extend prosperity to her like a
river,
and the wealth of the nations like an overflowing
stream;
and you shall suck, you shall be carried upon her
hip,
and dandled upon her knees.
As one whom his mother comforts,
So I will comfort you . . .
and your heart shall rejoice" (Is. 66:12-14).

Summary. If from this abundance of symbols one
truth emerges above all — and it does — this is
certainly the benevolent attitude and the loving care
with which Yahweh surrounds his people. But this
is not what really matters. God is merciful, he is
pure goodness and loves his creatures. It is more to
the point therefore that all these texts indicate the
great, personal love, which God directs to his
people. This is the great power which inspires all
his interventions. It is a love which chooses the
totally unmerited, which is spiritual, never merely
carnal; it possesses infinite fidelity toward the people
with which he made his covenant. — In the New
Testament, which uncovers the deepest sense of God's

fatherhood, this father love receives its full relevancy. The titles of shepherd and bridegroom are verified in the God-man who lived among us. By this they have become not only tangible, so that they have more meaning for us, but also enriched with a new element, self-sacrifice.

II

THE HUMAN RESPONSE

"You shall love the Lord your God
 . . . and your neighbor as yourself"

(Mk. 12:29-31)

A.

THE OLD TESTAMENT

One can distinguish several Old Testament stages
in the development of man's first and most important
religious duty to love God.

The oldest books use it only twice, in Exodus 20:6
and Judges 5:31. We merely mention these, because
the antiquity of both texts is uncertain and the exact
meaning of the expression "those who love me" is
not exactly clear.

In the second phase, encompassing the pre-exile
prophets, God increasingly reveals his holiness, his
justice, his universality and his abhorrence of sin.
All these attributes tend to portray the divine love
as personal, demanding and jealous. But the human
response did not measure up. The prophets from
Amos to Ezekiel are too preoccupied with Israel's

sinfulness and its rejection of Yahweh to even mention
a commandment of love. There is therefore a
recognizable delay in the exposition of this exalted
theme. The divine pedagogy saw fit not to reveal the
possibility of loving God before the end of the period
of the Kings. It first comes to light in Jeremiah 2:2:

> "I remember the devotion of your youth,
> Your love as a bride,
> how you followed me in the wilderness
> in a land not sown."

This heralds a new phase, the time of Deuteronomy, the book discovered in the temple in 622 (2
Kings 22). This presents the covenant as a revelation
of God's electing and faithful love. In this it follows
the prophet Hosea, but not entirely. Hosea indeed
speaks of Yahweh's love for Israel, but never of a
reciprocal love for him, neither as fact nor as duty;
Deuteronomy however also speaks of the love of the
people. In Hosea the love of God for Israel is as
that of a man for his wife (3:1) or of a father for
his son (11:1); in Deuteronomy one meets the father-
son relationship (8:5; 14:1 ff.) but never in connection
with love. More note-worthy still, there is not the
least trace of the marriage analogy.

If it is true that Deuteronomy depends on Hosea,
as is usually asserted, one must agree that it has
radically transformed his doctrine of love. This
virtue in Deuteronomy is demanding ("You must love
the Lord your God . . ."); it is closely allied to reverence and expresses itself in obedience to God's com-

mandments. In all the texts which mention love-in-return (6:5; 10:12; 11:1, 13, 22; 13:4; 19:9; 30:6, 16, 20) the immediate context speaks of obedience to the commandments and fidelity to the law. Over and over again the author repeats the same demands: walk the ways of God, keep his commandments to fear, serve, listen to and obey him. From this one can gather how closely love is connected with the law, which is precisely what the book wants to proclaim and propagate. This is strongly brought out in 13:3. After the prohibition against listening to false prophets, the author continues: "The Lord your God is testing you, to know whether you love the Lord your God and fear him and keep his commandments." Keeping the commandments is thus made the norm of love. In short, love is identified with fidelity to the covenant; one might therefore call it "covenant love."

There are many examples of this outside the Bible. The so-called letters of Amarna use the term to indicate the relationship between sovereign and vassal. Pharaoh is expected to love his vassals. The reverse is also true: "My lord, I, Zalat, love the king, my lord, so does the king of Nuhasse, the king of Nii . . . all these kings are servants of my lord." The vassal must love the Pharaoh; this is the formula determining his servitude. Rib Adda asks the same Pharaoh on the occasion of a colleague's desertion: "Must I who love perish?" (letter 114:68). Subjects must love their king. Rib Adda's faithful subjects are "those who love me" and these are placed opposite to traitors and deserters (83:51; 137:47).

The Bible itself copies this ancient Eastern terminology. Chiram calls King David his friend, because they have concluded a treaty (2 Sam. 5:11; 1 Kings 5:15). In 2 Samuel 19:6-7 Joab upbraids King David for being so concerned with the death of a rebellious son that he pays little attention to those who remained faithful to him. He accuses David that he "loves who hate him and hates who love him." Those who love him are his servants, as is clear from verse 6. 1 Samuel 18:16 says that "All Israel and Judah loved David, for he went out and came in before them." It is clear that the author mentions this as a factor which brings David a step nearer to the throne; the people are attached to him.

On the strength of this material from biblical and other sources, which portray love as imposed on the subjects in the sense of servitude and thus may be called "convenant fidelity," it seems justifiable to see the precepts of Deuteronomy in the same juridical sense. But if this is an acceptable explanation, it promptly faces a difficulty: Deuteronomy presents love for God in the form of a commandment: "You shall love the Lord your God with all your heart, and with all your soul, and with all your might" (6:5). How can one prescribe love, which is, by nature, a free and spontaneous expression? Other biblical texts mentioning the love of God present it as a fact: one does or does not loves him. Here it is ordered. The difficulty disappears entirely when one sees the demanded love as covenant fidelity, practically a precept to serve God and obey him.

This is confirmed in that Deuteronomy is preeminently the biblical document not restrictively of love, but of the covenant. More than other books, it sees love as analogous to the relationship of a vassal to his master. Its long list of maledictions and oaths, which refer to acceptance or rejection of the law, breathes this same juridical atmosphere.

Even the repetitive demand to love God "with your whole heart and your whole soul" (6:5; 10:12; 11:13; 13:4; 30:6) does not seem at variance with the above proposed view. In contrast with our usage of "soul," the Israelite understands this not as a part, but as the whole person; we too sometimes use the word in that sense, as, for example, when we speak of a town of so many souls (inhabitants). "Heart" for him means not just the seat of affection but the whole interior man. "With your whole heart and your whole soul" indicates man in his totality as a living and acting being. His whole personality is involved, not just a token sector of it. In short, Deuteronomy's love expresses itself in acts of adoration and obedience.

Thus one can better understand what Jesus later says: "He who loves me keeps my commandments" (Jn. 14:15; cf. 15:10; 1 Jn. 3:24; 5:2). It also becomes obvious why there is no breach of tradition when the post-exilic literature speaks so little of loving God.

In post-exile literatures, themes from the older books — love between bridegroom and bride, the commandment of love as such, etc. — have already

been established. The later psalms and prophets
avoid the expression "to love God"; they prefer to
accentuate attachment to the law or to wisdom (Ps.
119; 127; Sir. 4:14), which means making life with
and for God possible. This indicates a certain yearn-
ing in later Judaism for a more immediate relationship with its transcendent God.

We note that Old Testament man conceives of
God, above all, as his deliverer, his helper. He is
therefore not so much appreciated for his perfections
as for his assistance. Even in a somewhat sentimental
text like Deuteronomy 6:5, the commandment of
love is preceded by a reminder of the Lord's initiative: the people are urged to love "their" God, that
is to say him whom they must thank for their election
and deliverance.

Human love has value insofar as it is expressed
in practice. One loves God in reality only when one
serves him; without service there is no love. Such
service demands the commitment of the whole person; in biblical language, man is called upon "to
love with his whole heart, his whole soul and all
his might" (Deut. 6:5). Actually, it is self-abandon-
ment, total dedication of oneself to another. Remarkably, this is exactly what the Old Testament
describes as faith. The words "faith" and "love"
have entirely different emotional values, but their
objective content is very similar; the first demands
submission of one's whole being to God, the second
expresses itself in obedience. The human response
to God's love, which the Old Testament urges, is

not so much love-in-return as it is faith: faithful submission.

Besides the command to love God, the Old Testament also knows another: "You must love your neighbor as yourself" (Lev. 19:18). Neighbor here however is restricted to a tribal member, but interest for another is at least awakened. Early in the Scriptures enmity toward others is considered offensive to God (Gen. 3:12; 4:9); in the decalog, duties to God are immediately followed by duties toward the neighbor. In further development of the law, love of neighbor is extended to aliens who live in the country, not because of natural alliance, but for a salvific historical reason: Yahweh took the Israelites to his heart, when they themselves sojourned in Egypt as aliens (Lev. 19:34; Deut. 10:18). In later Judaism, the notion was further narrowed: it comprised only those aliens who were proselytes in the strict sense; foreigners and Samaritans were excluded (Mekilta Ex. 21:35), as were all non-pharisees by the pharisees (Billerbeck II 514-518). In Qumrân neighbor was limited to members of the community, because the decisive hour of the final time forbids association with the godless (I QS 1, 9). On the other hand, hellenistic Judaism in the diaspora extended the notion to include pagans; this was prompted by their sense of a world mission as well as by the influence of hellenistic humanitarian concepts (Sir. 13:15; Philo. De Virt. 103). The last step is taken when the wisdom teachers prescribe that one must forgive everyone, even one's enemies (Sir. 27:30-28:7).

Love for neighbor is measured by love for self ("as yourself," Lev. 18:19), the so-called golden rule. The prophets never tire of repeating that it is impossible to please God without reverence for one's neighbor. God condemns the heathens who stifle mercy (Amos 1:11). Love for one's neighbor has greater value than offering sacrifice (Hos. 4:2; 6:6); justice must be crowned by sincere love (Mic. 6:8). He who really wishes to fast must assist the poor, widows and orphans (Is. 58:6-12; Job 31:15-23).

B.

THE NEW TESTAMENT

The New Testament texts concerning our duty to love are built on the texts of the Old Testament. Here again love forms man's response to the redeeming love of God, this time as realized in the person and work of Jesus Christ. Here again the love for God is obedience rather than sentiment.

1. The **divine Master himself** teaches that our love for God must surpass all else. He cites the commandment of Deuteronomy 6:5: "Hear, oh Israel: The Lord our God, the Lord is one, and you shall love the Lord your God with all your heart, and with all your soul, and with all your mind and with all your strength" (Mk. 12:29, par.). He explains what he means: "No one can serve two masters: for either he will hate the one and love the other, or he will be devoted to one and despise the other. You cannot serve God and mammon" (Mt. 6:24, par.).

To love God is the same as to submit totally to him, serve him completely, "to seek first his kingdom and his righteousness" (Mt. 6:33), even if it brings with it revilement, persecution, or even death (Mt. 5:10-12, par.). The Master exemplifies this in the case of sinful woman who pours ointment over him in the house of the pharisee: "I tell you her sins, which are many, are forgiven, for she loved much" (Lk. 7:47). A little further on, this love is called faith: "Your faith has saved you: go in peace" (v. 50). Insofar as the love of God implies faithful docility, Jesus remains completely within the Old Testament context.

What the Savior actually corrects in the Old Law is the love for neighbor. The restatement is so drastic that he could say, "A new commandment I give you, that you love one another" (Jn. 13:34). Here, in the first place, the **central position** is new. In Christianity love of one's neighbor is the main commandment, if not the only commandment, the directive of all human action and the sum of all perfection (Mt. 22:39); the supporting foundation of Jewish ethics however was not love but justice, to which the love for one's neighbor and many other ethical and cultural commandments belongs. — Furthermore, its avowedly **religious character** is new. It is not only placed next to love of God, but it is most intimately connected with it: "And a second is like it, you shall love your neighbor as yourself. On these two commandments depend all the law and the prophets" (Mt. 22:39, par.). It is clear that Jesus

sees both commandments as a unit. Love for one's
neighbor has its ground in love for God; in its turn,
it is a guarantee for the sincerity of this love for
God. Neither can exist without the other. Love for
one's neighbor, detached from its divine ground
shrivels to pure humanism. Recognizing that God,
the Father of all peoples, is the perfect love, man
enters into a new relationship with his neighbor, because loving one's neighbor means following God's
example. — So we come to the third feature of
Christian love of neighbor: its new **motive.** The
synagogue too prescribed charity, but it did this with
profit in mind; by dropping the notion of reward,
Jesus abolishes the quantitative criterion (the size of
the gift); by pointing to the example of his Father
(Lk. 6:36), he raises love to a qualitative level residing
in the will itself. The word **neighbor** also acquires a
new meaning. True, Jesus does not furnish a theoretical description of it, but neither does he demand,
with the Hellenes, a general love for humanity. In
the parable of the Samaritan he intends to express
how real love for one's neighbor operates. It does
not question the person, nationality or religion of
the other; every person who needs our help is our
neighbor, and we his. It therefore includes our enemies. Love for adversaries (probably concerning law-
suits, Mt. 5:38) and for enemies (probably enemies of
the new people of God, i.e. persecutors Mt. 5:43)
should not express itself only in a negative way
through toleration or foregoing revenge (Mt. 5:38-42),
but in a positive way through assisting him when
necessary (Mt. 5:43-48), and forgiving him without

any limitations (Mt. 18:21; Lk. 17:4). Here the negative (and therefore limiting) formulation of the traditional golden rule (Lev. 19:18) is abandoned and replaced by a positive command, enormously enlarging love's field of work: "Whatever you wish that men would do to you, do so to them" (Mt. 7:12; Lk. 6:31). The divine perfection thus displayed in acting toward even an enemy (Mt. 5:48) does not make the faithful into demi-gods or supermen; in such acts of love performed by his followers Jesus simply sees a partial manifestation of God's own perfect mercy (Lk. 6:36).

One consequence of this high estimation of the love for neighbor is that even religious duties must give way to it, such as offering of sacrifices (Mt. 5:23) and celebration of the Sabbath (Mk. 3:1-6; Lk. 13:10-17). Jesus especially disliked the heartless formalism of the lawyers; they followed ritual precepts scrupulously, but they trampled down the humane aspect (Mt. 23:23). In contrast to their cold, externally correct regard for the law, Jesus refers (Mt. 9:13) to the word of the prophet Hosea (6:6): Go and teach them what "I desire steadfast love and not sacrifice" means. The special significance of love for neighbor is further underlined in the description of the last judgment (Mt. 25:31-46), where works of mercy are exclusively mentioned.

From all this one may conclude that love for one's neighbor really differs from all other forms of love: from erôs as coveting and thus, in fact, egoistic; from friendship founded on natural sympathy, stimu-

lated only by natural qualities and extending itself
only to those who are like-minded; from a fanatic,
purely theoretical love for mankind, and so on. In
practice, "a neighbor" is he whom God allows to
come into our lives, and no one else. Jesus insists
that we love this person — irrespective of our sentiment or inclination — in service. And this is far from
easy.

The great stumbling block for our love of others
is without doubt our innate self-love and the effects
of the original sin, which weigh us down. In order
to love another sincerely, we need strong motives
to which we can constantly return. Jesus provides
these. First is his own explicit order: "This is my
commandment, that you love one another" (Jn. 15:12,
17). We must see this in the solemn context, in which
he announces it. The parting speech (Jn. 13-17)
wherein his words are recorded is, in a way, his
testament — the testament of his heart. Its dominant
theme is his prayer to the Father, "That all may be
one, as You, Father, in Me and I in You" (Jn. 17:21).
The last will of a father is always sacred to his
children. How much more so is the testament of one
whom we must thank for everything! Another motive
is the example of our heavenly Father, who makes
the sun rise upon the bad and the good (Mt. 5:45);
our love too must go out to all men, even our
enemies (v. 44). He who loves only his friends, does
nothing special; Jesus specifically demands something
extraordinary (v. 46), an absolute and altruistic love
(Lk. 6:34). To the question of the scribe, "Who is

my neighbor" the Master replies with the beautiful parable of the charitable Samaritan, who came to the rescue of an enemy in trouble (Lk. 10). No one has ever given a more striking example of this love for the distressed than the Master himself. Luke, the evangelist of mercy, especially draws our attention to it. According to him Jesus regarded in a special way the socially dispossessed of his time, the poor (Lk. 4:18; 7:22), the women and foreigners. Spiritual pariahs, publicans and sinners find a friend in him (7:34) and he does not shrink from visiting them (5:27, 30; 15:1; 19:7). The strongest motive, finally, will always be that we see our Master in our neighbor: "As you did it to one of the least of these my brethren, you did it to me" (Mt. 25:40).

2. Where the Master gave the example, his disciples followed. We see this clearly in **Paul**. God's love for him demands a response. As the Master refers to the first and greatest commandment, so too the apostle insists on a direct love of God (2 Thess. 3:5; 1 Cor. 2:9; 8:3; Rom. 8:28). This love in turn must also go out to Christ: "If any one has no love for the Lord, let him be accursed" (1 Cor. 16:22). "Grace be with all who love our Lord Jesus Christ with love undying" (Eph. 6:24). From Philemon we hear that he loves the Lord Jesus (Philem. 5 and 7). Above all the apostle himself is filled with the love of Christ (Philem. 3:4-9). Thus Paul speaks indeed of love for God, but he does this seldom, and nowhere uses a direct demand to love God. He himself gives the reason in the two texts quoted above.

There the active form of love (of man) is followed
closely by a passive form, and thus man's activity
is shifted to God. The apostle's personal experience
is reflected in fact in these amplifications, by which
his life and his doctrine are formed. The sentence,
"We know that in everything God works for good,
with those who love him," becomes absolutely Pauline
through the addition of, "who are called according
to his purpose" (Rom. 8:28). We see the same in 1
Cor. 8:3. After the beginning of the sentence, "If
one loves God," the reader might expect, "he has
known God"; but Paul evidently feels that this
gives too much credit to man, and he therefore places
the consequent in the passive voice: "he is known
by God." Because God first rested his loving eye
upon him, he is given the ability to respond with
love from his side. Faith therefore is the first response to God's salvific gift (Gal. 2:19); it becomes
active in love (Gal. 5:6). I believe in the love of
God (of Jesus) for me — this is the fundamental
creed of the Christian. How closely Paul approaches
John in this is apparent from the words, "In this is
love, not that we loved God, but that he loved us"
(1 Jn. 4:10).

The human answer to God's inviting love is usually
formulated differently, namely through the love
for one's neighbor. "Walk in love, as Christ loved
us and gave himself up for us, a fragrant offering
and sacrifice to God" (Eph. 5:2). Possibly, this
completely selfless love of Christ was used as a
model for the beautiful Canticle of Love in 1

Corinthians 13. In 12:31 Paul writes of a royal way, much higher than the mental powers in which they glory, namely love (exactly what is lacking in them). Obviously he is himself seized by the Holy Spirit, whose gifts he has previously mentioned, because he spontaneously intones a hymn of love as beautiful and sublime, as any ever written. We quote the text in its entirety.

1   If I speak in the tongues of men and of angels, but have not love,
    I am a noisy gong or a clanging cymbal.

2   And if I have prophetic powers, and understand all mysteries and all knowledge,
    and if I have all faith, so as to remove mountains, but have not love, I am nothing.

3   If I give away all I have, and if I deliver my body to be burned,
    but have not love, I gain nothing.

4   Love is patient and kind; love is not jealous or boastful;

5   it is not arrogant or rude.
    Love does not insist on its own way; it is not irritable or resentful;

6   it does not rejoice at wrong,
    but rejoices in the right.

7   Love bears all things, believes all things,
    hopes all things, endures all things.

8   Love never ends;
    as for prophecies, they will pass away;

as for tongues, they will cease;
as for knowledge, it will pass away.

9   For our knowledge is imperfect
and our prophecy is imperfect;

10 but when the perfect comes,
the imperfect will pass away.

11 When I was a child, I spoke like a child,
I thought like a child, I reasoned like a child;
when I became a man,
I gave up childish ways.

12 For now we see in a mirror dimly,
but then face to face.
Now I know in part; then I shall understand fully,
even as I have been fully understood.

13 So faith, hope, love abide, these three;
but the greatest of these is love.

The apostle here extols, not a humanistic philan-
thropy but a supernatural love for neighbor. This
same virtue, which regulates behavior toward others
(4-7), is mentioned in one breath with faith and
hope (13). Thus it is one of the three great theological
virtues, obviously because in the neighbor one loves
God himself. The poem is composed of three stanzas:

a. Love is indispensable (1-3). Without it, every
charism and every practice of virtue, even raised
to the highest degree, is without value. Three times
this is expressed in a refrain: I serve no earthly
purpose (1), I am nothing (2), I am of no avail (3).
In other words: only he who loves is a real Christian.

b.   Attributes of love (4-7), first the negative (4-6), then the positive (7). Here the countenance of love is unveiled and personified as the virtue; it reminds us of the countenance of Christ, insofar as he is presented to the readers as a model they must follow. His characteristics are, one by one, worthy of meditation.

c.   Permanent duration of love (8-13). While love, which resides in the will, never perishes, (8a) prophecy, speaking of languages and doctrinal knowledge, all belonging to the mind, shall pass away. Only love abides in the life hereafter; our total spiritual dowry — faith and hope included — reaches only as far as the grave. Only he who possesses love has eternal life, and he has it already here on earth.

The apostle himself presents a paraphrase of the centerpiece of this canticle in Romans 12:9-21, there rather in the form of a direct admonition. The Master said: "On these two commandments (the love for God and for the neighbor) depends the whole law and the prophets"; the disciple in his turn attests, "Any other commandment is summed up in this sentence. You shall love your neighbor as yourself. Love causes the neighbor no evil; for that reason it fulfills the whole law" (Rom. 13:8; Gal. 5:13; 6:2). From this it is clear, that the apostle sees our love for God displayed in our love of others.

Love is a gift of God (1 Thess. 3:12; 2 Thess. 3:5), a power imparted by the Trinity. It is the fruit of the Spirit (Gal. 5:22; Rom. 5:5; 15:30), has God as

its teacher (1 Thess. 4:9) and model (Eph. 5:1), is
the law of Christ referring to the word and example
of Christ (Rom. 15:2; 2 Cor. 8:9; 10:1; Philem. 2:5;
Col. 3:13); this is the doctrine of the apostle of the
gentiles.

3. As we have seen, Jesus is for **John** light and
life or, if you prefer, revealer and redeemer. Christian existence is thus determined through **faith** in
the Lord, which offers eternal life. By "believing"
(used 98 times in his gospel, 9 times in his first letter)
the evangelist expresses total personal relationship
with Christ, which includes an intellectual element
("believing that," 6:69; 8:24; 9:18 . . .) and trustful
surrender ("believing in Jesus," 3:16, 18, 36; 6:29 . . .).
John sees the object of this faith as nothing other
than the person of the God-man Christ. One uncon-
ditionally surrenders to him, because one believes
in his word — he believes that the Lord is what he
professes to be: the Son, who is sent, who is one
with the Father; the food, the light of the world, the
definitive revelation of God — in a word, the Mediator. Because the Christian believes in Jesus' divine
mission, he believes "in him"; because he accepts
his words and works as the unveiling of divine reality,
he entrusts himself to him (12:44).

This faith in the Lord includes a loving and mutual
knowledge. "This is eternal life, that they know thee,
the only true God, and Jesus Christ whom thou hast
sent" (17:3, 23). "I am the good shepherd. I know
my own and my own know me, as the Father knows
me and I know the Father" (10:14). This complete

belief and deep religious knowledge is the source of a most intimate relationship between the Christian and Jesus and the Father, which John often formulates as "being one in the Lord" (17:21-26) or "remaining in him" (15:4-8; 8:31; 6:56) and in his love (15:10); in reverse, he is in the believer (17:23), the Father and he himself shall make their abode in him (14:23).

John knows only two Christian commandments in the real sense, faith and **love**. This agapè is the love of Christians for each other: "This is my commandment, that you love one another as I have loved you" (15:12; cf. 13:34; 15:17; 1 Jn. 2:7-11; 3:11-23; 4:7-5:4; 2 Jn. 5). Brotherly love is the Christian commandment par excellence. How it can be recognized John does not say in so many words. One may think of humble service (13:15; cf. 1 Jn. 3:17), but only to the extent that he is ready to give his life for another (15:13). Any further specifications of its object, its deeds and requirements are actually contained within the great commandment itself, again and again commended to the reader as an ideal rule of life and existence. According to John, one cannot understand brotherly love unless one starts from the love of the Father for us, in and through the Son. The divine agapè in its eternal fullness is the source and model of every other love. The Father loves the Son (3:35; 5:20; 10:17; 15:9a, 10b; 17:34, 26); as the Father loves the Son, so the Son loves the faithful (13:1, 34; 15:9, 12); as the Son loves the faithful, so they must love each other (13:34; 15:12). For John the new and

specifically Christian aspect of the commandment of
love is the fact that the divine love is motivation and
model for our love. Jesus brought the commandment, but over and above this he brought himself;
only through the incarnation could we know "God
is love" and loves us (17:23, 26; cf. 1 Jn. 4:8, 16); the
line therefore is vertical, coming down from above.
As for the entire salvific work, John stresses the divine
initiative on this central point. He sees a second
specifically Christian trait in the creative power of
the divine agapè which transforms the interior of
man and nourishes and directs his relations with the
brethren. Brotherly love is therefore an active and
vital participation in the love of the Father for us
in Christ; it is a continuation of this divine love in
our relations with others. Christians, favored with
the active presence of the Father and Son, love each
other with the same divine love and form a unity
comparable with the unity of the divine Persons
(17:21-23). In love for the brethren the divine love-
force reveals itself in us, and reaches its complete
expression (1 Jn. 4:12). Love for the Creator and
for his children are inseparably connected (5:1);
this is John's interpretation of the word of Jesus
concerning the first commandment and the second
which is like it (Mt. 22:39, par.).

How, finally, do these two commandments of faith
and love stand with regard to one another? The
loving saving will of God generates and nourishes
man's response. In its composition there is a commandment of love, an imperative; this is only made

possible by a corresponding indicative: "Beloved, if God so loved us, we also ought to . . ." — here we might be inclined to continue with "love God" but John says, ". . . ought to love one another" (1 Jn. 4:11). In the preceding verse he had already said, "In this is love, not that we loved God but that he loved us . . ." We are expected to accept this love by believing in it. From Jesus the divine love-force extends over all who "believe in love" which God has given us by sending us his Son (1 Jn. 4:14-16; cf. 16:27; 17:25). That faith in Christ is necessary for attainment of the divine love is obvious from the fact that both are presented as one commandment: "And this is his commandment, that we should believe in the name of his Son Jesus Christ and love one another just as he commanded us" (1 Jn. 3:23). We will return to this in our synthesis.

4. The remainder of the New Testament does not add much to what we have already quoted. The Acts of the Apostles offer two descriptions of the early Christian community (2:42-47 and 4:32-35) which actually demonstrate that the preaching of the apostles was not in vain and the fire which Jesus brought to earth was not extinguished. The word love does not occur in it, and yet it was so strongly at work among the first Christians, that it led to community of goods; outwardly, it manifested the zeal and unity for which the Lord prayed in his parting sermon. The admonitions to brotherly love in the first letter of Peter are simple, but intimate.

He writes: "Having purified your souls by your obedience to the truth for a sincere love of the brethren, love one another earnestly from the heart, as people who have been born anew" (1:22). With a clear allusion to the Sermon on the Mount, he gives practical advice: "Finally, all of you, have unity of spirit, sympathy, love of the brethren, a tender heart and a humble mind. Do not return evil for evil or reviling for reviling; but on the contrary bless, for to this you have been called, that you may obtain a blessing" (3:8). And in 4:8 he insists: "Above all hold unfailing your love for one another, since love covers a multitude of sins . . ."

When James writes that faith without works is dead (2:17; cf. Gal. 5:6), he concurs with Paul, because he has the works of charity in mind. He stresses the need for brotherly love, which manifests itself toward every one (2:1-16), including the poor man clad in rags (2:2) — for God has chosen him too as heir of the Kingdom. This love is an act of faith because it is demanded by faith, made possible through faith and accounted as justice through faith (2:14). The commandment of love is "the royal law" (2:8), which is the first and greatest commandment of the Kingdom of God, embracing also those who, in the eyes of the world, are poor and lowly, but in reality are rich in faith (2:5).

III

ATTEMPT AT SYNTHESIS

"Ubi caritas, ibi Deus"

1. Description of love

The Bible indicates the primacy of love with convincing power. In determining a reason for Yahweh's salvific acts in Israel, the Old Testament continually insists on his inexhaustible and gracious love; the New Testament does the same, when it speaks of God's salvation works in Christ. In return, the faithful accept love for one another and for God as the first and greatest commandment. For John, brotherly love is the new commandment (13:34; 1 Jn. 2:7), the distinguishing mark of true disciples (13:35). For Paul it is the first fruits of the Spirit, the foundation and epitome of all virtues (Gal. 5:22; 1 Cor. 13:4-7; Col. 3:12-14), the root and crown of Christian life (Rom. 5:1-5; Eph. 3:17-19; cf. 1 Pet. 4:8). It is therefore important that we have a correct concept of salvation history. It seems methodically advisable that we restrict ourselves to the New Testament which, as is evident from the preceding analysis of love, built upon the Old and brought it to perfection.

Religious agapè-love is always and everywhere

unselfish and active. Benevolence, altruism and
activity are three facets of love as it is revealed.

Divine — this means Christian — love is above all
benevolent; it always has the welfare of another
in view and rejoices in it. It is altruistic because it
is diametrically opposed to self-centeredness; more
than this, it is prepared to sacrifice all egoism for
the welfare of another. Thus God loves men and
does not spare even his only Son (Rom. 8:32; Jn. 3:16;
1 Jn. 4:9); Christ loves them and gives his life for
them (Rom. 8:33); the Christian too must lay down
his life for his neighbor (Jn. 15:12). Finally, it is
active benevolence, not purely emotional but express-
ing itself in deeds. This is true also in extreme cases.
Even love for persecutors must at least show itself
in prayer and in love for God (the infinitely Perfect,
to whose happiness we can add nothing) through
obedience.

Two qualities still deserve mention. The first is
universality; this flows from altruism. Because it is
not self-seeking, it has no reason to restrict itself to
those from whom it expects something or for whom
it has preference. For this reason Christian love
excludes no one, not even persecutors. When the
New Testament on occasion speaks of love for the
enemy — which it seldom does (Mt. 5:44-47; Rom.
12:14, 22) — this is not meant for daily use, but it
does underline the universality of love ("If you
salute only your brethren . . . Mt. 5:47).

Finally, love is by nature mutual, but not in the

sense that one loves only those who show love in
return. The New Testament distinguishes between
those who reject love and those who accept it. True
love to be fruitful must be mutual. Accepted love,
which succeeds in attaining the good it has in view,
is active; rejected love is not. Therefore the New
Testament speaks especially of brotherly love, seldom
of love for outsiders, never of love for the damned.

2. God's plan for us

God's love for us is the directive decree of his
sovereign will regarding the world and its salvation.
His purpose is to allow us to share in his own life
and to lead us into the intimacy of the three divine
Persons (Eph. 1:3-14). God's fatherhood becomes
reality for man in the true and unique sonship of
him who is the Son by nature. Union or identification
of men with the Son is the work of the Spirit of the
Son, who descends into them to effect this from
within.

God's fatherhood, understood in a Christian sense,
was entirely unknown before Christ's coming. When
Greek and Roman myths ascribe strict fatherhood
to a god over other gods, this portrayed true fatherhood, but not true God. Usually however, divine
fatherhood was understood figuratively. God was
father in his capacity of creator of the universe,
or — as with the Jews — by virtue of a covenant
which exalted him to the status of king. As such
he showed a fatherly love for his creature or for
his subjects. But all this was, and remained, meta-
phorical.

In the New Testament God is never called Father simply because he is "fatherly." He is truly **the** Father: Christ calls him his Father, the disciples their Father. He is never called father of all men, still less father of all things. Certainly, he will come to be known as the father of all men, but only when all men become Christ's followers. To become a child of God, one must be born of God (1 Jn. 2:29; 3:9; 4:7; 5:1, 18) and that means much more than just being a creature. It is a birth which imparts a new and eternal life, which comes from God, a birth which imprints in us a likeness to God. This divine fatherhood therefore, which effects our spiritual rebirth, makes us partakers of his divine life.

God realized his plan by sending One, who obviously is much more than the popularly expected messianic Savior (Lk. 2:11); he is his only begotten Son, whom he loves with an infinite love, who rests upon his breast and is himself God. With the pledge of his love, which surpasses the value of man to an unimaginable degree, God's generosity has reached its zenith in salvation history, for in this Son he has given us everything. He allows him to become man, to die for us on the cross (Rom. 5:8; 8:32; 1 Jn. 4:10) and after his earthly life placed him at our disposal for ever (Mt. 28:20; Jn. 14:18 . . .). Jesus on his part has revealed himself through word and bearing, through works and wonders as God's only Son and the perfect image of his Father. Therefore union with the Son means, for us, union with the Father. God is no longer far away; as one of us he has made his abode with us. The drama of the divine love enacts itself in and through the Person of Jesus Christ's life; the union between God and man is executed in him according to his last prayer (Jn. 17). John and Paul clearly describe how this union with Christ takes place. The former uses the metaphor of a vine; the branches draw their life sap from it and can only bear fruit while they remain connected with the vine. Paul develops the metaphor of a human body in which the members are different but nevertheless form one whole, directed, moved and maintained by the head. We are "in Christ" (John says "in his love") or, simply, "Christ." Through this equalization with him we become sons, because God's Son has come to make us "adopted children" and for this purpose the Father sent the Spirit of his Son into our hearts, permitting us to address him as "Abba, Father" (Rom. 8).

Through this divine intervention the relationship between God and man is radically changed: it is no longer mere sympathy between Creator and creature, Master and servant; it is a love-relationship between father and child. Christianity leads man into the intimacy of God. God loves the Christian in his Son (Eph. 1:6), with the same love with which he loves his only Son (Jn. 17:26). The union of Christian with God is, like that of the Son with the Father, one of pure love (Jn. 17). Childlike love for God is the first commandment of the new religion: Christianity is, in essence, love.

God's plan is reducible to the fact that he offered

to share his love, which is his own life with us. He
has sent his Son to enable us to lead his divine
life in union with him (Jn. 1:9). This divine life is
one of love (v. 11), precisely because God's inner
life, his Trinitarian life, is a life of loving. So it is
Jesus Christ who reveals and brings the love of God.
In him we have simultaneously a gift and a task:
above all a gift indeed, but also a duty.

3.   The human response

Man must accept God's offer. How can he do
that? Through **faith** in Christ, John and Paul answer
(1 Jn. 4:16; Gal. 2:19), in keeping with Old Testament
tradition. Through the faith man receives Christ's
life and is incorporated into Christ to continue his
life of love and sacrifice. To believe is not only
a beginning act; it is an attitude toward life. Reborn
as child of God, the believer must love his Father in
and through God's gift of love, Jesus Christ. In this
connection, it is noteworthy that Paul and John do
speak of our faith in Christ and God, but very
seldom of our **love** for God (John does this only once).
When Paul does so, he understands this love for
God not as duty but as an endowment for which
we must thank God's generosity. "We know that
in everything God works for good with those who
love him, who **are called** according to his purpose"
(Rom. 8:28). Or, clearer, in 1 Corinthians 8:3: "But
if one loves God, one is known by him"; in other
words, we can actively turn ourselves to God only insofar as we are receptive to him. (The same concept
of passive and active love is seen in Gal. 4:9; 1 Cor.

13:12). Elsewhere this divine initiative is emphatically emphasized in the words, "God's love has been poured into our hearts . . ." (Rom. 5:5). Paul teaches the first effect of divine love is not that our love returns to God, but that those who receive it are prepared to give their lives in service of the neighbor (Gal. 5:13). The reason for this undoubtedly lies in the fact that love, in the New Testament, means active love. But an active love for God, who is infinitely happy in himself and needs nothing from us, is not easy to imagine. Paul therefore places love for God in the background, and John mentions it only once. We believe in God; this is our love-response. Through this faith we become children of God.

4. Realization of God's plan

God has the first word. His love is a gift and we accept it in faith. This demands total submission to God, and seeks an outlet in a life of brotherly love (Paul: Gal. 5:6; Jn. first letter 4:7-12; Jas., 2nd chapter).

But why love the neighbor? Jesus himself gives the reply: to imitate the heavenly Father, who loves every one and lets the rain come down upon the good and the bad (Mt. 5:45-48; Lk. 6:36); peacemakers are called "children of God" (Mt. 5:9); later he will point to his own example (Mt. 20:25-28). Another reason is that brotherly love is, in essence, the law and the prophets (Mt. 7:12).

According to Paul, Christians must imitate the Father in his love. But more clearly than the gospels

he says that one who imitates Christ, the figure of
God (Col. 1:15) also imitates God: "Be imitators of
God, as beloved children. And walk in love as
Christ has loved us, and gave himself up for us a
fragrant offering and sacrifice to God" (Eph. 5:1-2).
Paul and the synoptics consider brotherly love as
the summation of all Christian duties: "He who loves
his neighbor has fulfilled the law" (Rom. 13:8, 10);
"the whole law is fulfilled in one word, You shall
love your neighbor as yourself" (Gal. 5:14; 6:2).

John teaches the same. As the Father loves the
Son and the Son his disciples so the disciples must
love each other (Jn. 17:23,26). "This is my commandment that you love one another as I have loved you"
(Jn. 15:12). By loving as God does himself, the child
is like his father. This likeness is not purely external,
but shows that one is born of God (1 Jn. 4:7 ff.),
because he makes such love possible from above.
The apostle of love also clearly suggests that the
whole law is fulfilled in one single commandment:
"This is my commandment, that you love one another"
(Jn. 15:17).

From the above we can draw three conclusions.
For the synoptics, as well as for Paul and John, a
Christian must imitate the love of his heavenly
Father. According to the same witnesses, he does
this when he imitates Christ's love, as manifested
in his whole life. All three sources further agree that
this love is the sum total of our duties and makes
us sharers in God's life.

One therefore who loves unselfishly, universally and actively, lives the life of God. For this reason Paul rates brotherly love higher than faith: "So faith, hope, love abide, these three; but the greatest of these is love." Why? Because faith opens us to accept the divine life, but love makes us actually share in it.

Since brotherly love is the undeniable expression of the divine life in Christians, it is at the same time the way God lives visibly in the world of today. He has sent us his Son to bring us his love. The Son no longer lives visibly among us. But his members in the world, we, who continue his love, make God tangible in this world.

A practical question, naturally is asked here: Whom must we love? or rather, must we love all people equally?

The New Testament clearly categorizes those who come under God's love. Christians, who accept his love, are loved by God completely. For those who do not accept his love, the New Testament does not even use the word. God's benevolence is shown them; this is an invitation that they also become his children. Christians are indeed his children; he loves them in the only ultimate object of his love, his Son Jesus Christ, of whom they are the members. Non-christians are not yet members of his Son, so he cannot yet love them fully. Or rather, his love is offered to them, but before they have been taken up in Christ, it does not reach them completely.

Christians imitate God's love, which above all demands perfect love for their fellow-Christians, since God is loved through them. Love for Christ's members is love for Christ himself. He identifies himself with them: "Truly, as you did it to the least of these, you did it to me" (Mt. 25:35-40). Only this equalization can bring us to feed and clothe our fellow-Christians. When Jesus declares that he who accepts his disciples, accepts him, he adds: "and he who welcomes me, welcomes him who sent me" (Mk. 9:39).

Paul speaks more of love for fellow-Christians than for other people. "Let us then, as we have opportunity, do good to all men, and especially to these, who are of the household of the faith" (Gal. 6:10). His main point is that just as love for the neighbor formerly consisted in helping members of the Old Covenant, so now it is service to the members of the New Covenant, care for the welfare of the new people of God (cf. 1 Thess. 4:9; Col. 1:4; Philem. 5; Eph. 4:1-6; 6:23). The words "Beloved" and "Brother" are interchangeable (1 Thess. 2:8; Phil. 5:1; Philem. 16).

Paul placed brotherly love in a central position, because the community of God belongs to the **end time** (Gal. 6:10; Rom. 13:11), between cross and parousia. It stands under the sign of the cross. It means readiness to serve and sacrifice, to forgive and respect, to cooperate and sympathize with the building up of the community (Gal. 5:24-26; 1 Cor. 13:4; etc.); it owes its entire existence to the mercy of God and the sacrificial death of the Anointed One. For

himself, the apostle makes it his task and his
highest ideal to imitate Christ in what he did and
suffered for the Church. He accepts his participation
in the suffering of Christ for the sake of the Church
(2 Cor. 1:3; Col. 1:24). The activity of God and man
become one in love. This builds up (1 Cor. 8:1),
it builds the future, it stands under the sign of the
end time: this is the great truth of 1 Corinthians 13.
It is a heavenly gift above all intellectual gifts, the
"royal way" which is more excellent than faith and
hope. These carry the marks of this imperfect world
but "love abides for ever," for it possesses everlasting
value.

John speaks exclusively of brotherly love. A
typical characteristic of the Jesus-figure as presented
in the synoptics, love for sinners, is entirely absent
in John. The synoptics show the Redeemer seeking
and rescuing the lost, and taking special interest in
sinners and publicans; John presents him as the
Good Shepherd, who gives his life for the sheep.
John does not divide people into the just and sinners, but into believers and unbelievers. Jesus' task is
to show the difference between the children of God
and the children of damnation. Hence the community of the brothers is a rather firmly closed one,
where brotherly love reigns. In 1 John **koinônia** (community) is a favorite word for the religious community within which the Christian dwells. To be a
Christian means to be united with God — with the
Father and the Son (1 Jn. 1:3, 6; Paul mentions only
communion with the Son) and this in turn means
union with the brethren, the believers. This is why

John is interested only in brotherly love. (He feels love of God is accomplished by love of neighbor).

As the Father loves the Son, so the Son loves the disciples (Jn. 15:9). They must respond to this love, not by loving him in return, but by keeping his commandments (chap. 14); and this obedience attests to their love for him. But he has only one commandment: brotherly love. By fulfilling this they will remain in his love. In John therefore we find a consistent theme. The Father loves the Son and commands him to love us. By obeying, the Son shows how much the Father loves us and at the same time returns love to the Father. The Son in turn commands us to love one another according to his example and thus grounds us in love; through our mutual love we love Christ in return and in him the Father.

The apostle of love nowhere mentions direct love for God (though he surely implies it); he speaks constantly of love which reaches God through neighbor. The synoptics do the same. Matthew points to love for God only at the end of his gospel: "This is the first and greatest commandment. And the second is like it: You shall love your neighbor as yourself" (Mt. 22:37). For what other reason could he assert that this second is like the first, than that our love for our neighbor is the measure of our love for God?

5. The means of bringing God's plan to realization

God's plan was to make man share in his love and life by incorporating him with his Son. This takes place through faith in the Word-made-man. Radically, man is saved when God's love is infused into him along with the divine life; in fact, this does not yet save him; since all life must diffuse itself, the life of love must do the same. Infused love is therefore both gift and task, it is indicative as well as imperative (the old man is undone — and must be undone: Col. 3:10; Eph. 4:22; one has put on Christ and must assume obligations: Gal. 3:27; Rom. 13:14; one puts on the new man and must do more and more: Col. 3:10, 12).

This task imposed by the imperative is the source of great difficulty. In a reborn man a center of opposition remains, a kind of fifth column: his nature still inclines to sin. His former offenses have been forgiven, his concupiscence has been counter-balanced by the power of grace, but his state remains precarious because of the pulling force of his sinful inclinations — the "old man" as Paul calls it. He can sin again, and thus separate himself from, and place himself in opposition to, God. This might take the form of love of pleasure (money, senses, etc.) or self-glorification (pride, disobedience, etc.); in any event, it is self-love. To be able to love others this must be overcome — and this calls for real effort. True love demands sacrifices, not just of gifts but of the person himself; true love, in its highest degree, demands one's life (Jn. 15:13).

Here we touch the heart of the imperative; no life of love is possible without sacrifice. For man inclined to sin this is truly difficult. Add to this

the fact that as a Christian he has an obligation to
imitate his Master, and that this Master has given
his life for him. He demands that we love one
another as he has loved us (Jn. 15:12). He insists
that we take him as our model — Paul says "put on
Christ" like a garment (Gal. 3:27). Jesus indicates
that his great commandment of love is the only way
to follow him ("this is my commandment," cf. Paul
in 1 Cor. 13:1-3). He also says that we can be
saved only by losing our lives, sacrificing ourselves
(Mt. 10:39, par.), and that we must leave everything
to carry our cross after him. This insistence on self-
denial is not a second commandment: the Lord im-
poses only one on us, **his** commandment, love of
neighbor. This makes it clear that these two coin-
cide: love for neighbor is self-denial. Christ himself
is the perfect example of this (Eph. 5:2; Phil. 2:5-8).
Paul teaches that love for another amounts to
"crucifying" the passions (Gal. 5:22-24).

We may perhaps present it in this way. The love
which God has for his Son, and in which we share,
is preferential, directed exclusively to Jesus. This is
the meaning of the parable of the guilty tenants in
the vineyard of "the beloved Son" (Mk. 12:5; cf. Mt.
12:18). His human vocation is to go to the end of the
way which the prophets traveled before him and on
which they died. The beloved Son is the martyr
who stands at the turning point of time, whose
death brings judgment on the world and founds a
new order (Mk. 12:8). He is the founder of the
new people of God (v. 10 ff.); one's attitude toward
him determines whether or not he will share in the

coming world. Hence faith is the factor which decides whether this "stumbling stone," Christ, brings salvation or damnation (Rom. 9:32; 1 Pet. 2:6-8; cf. Lk. 2:34); and faith is submission of the whole person. Service of the poorest brother is equal to service of the Son of Man and lack of love is equivalent to scorn for him. On the last day he shall judge both (Mt. 25:31-46). For that reason too Jesus calls the disciples who will suffer persecution for his sake blessed (Lk. 6:22). Hence he demands unconditional loyalty to his Person, loyalty unto death (Mt. 10:37, par.).

Love and suffering both belong to the essence of our Christian life; this is taught, as regards suffering, in Philippians 1:29; 2 Timothy 3:12; Acts 14:22. They have their intersection in the Founder of our holy religion. Through our suffering and our love we share in his life; or rather, he carries on his suffering and love in us. There is one great difference however: Christ suffered **out of** love, we suffer usually **through** love. In us it requires tolerance, great humility and adjustment, renunciation of self-interest and a continuous self-denial. But as his suffering out of love brought Christ to his glory (Lk. 24:36; Phil. 2:6-11), so our suffering through love will lead us to and with him in glory (Rom. 8:17; 2 Cor. 4:10, 17). This is the ideal Christian course of life.

"God is love;
and he who abides in love, abides in God
and God abides in him."

(1 Jn. 4:16)

A SELECT BIBLIOGRAPHY

A. WORKS OF REFERENCE

Quell-Stauffer, article "Agapao" in *Theologisches Worter-buch zum Neuen Testament* I, 20-55

Bijbels Woordenboek (Roermond 1957)

Vocabulaire biblique (Neuchatel 1956)

Vocabulaire de théologie biblique (Paris 1962)

Lexikon für Theologie und Kirche

E. Jacob: *Théologie de l'Ancien Testament* (Neuchatel 1955) 86-90; 163-175; 226-240

B. MONOGRAPHS

Cl. Wiéner: "Recherches sur l'amour pour Dieu dans l'Ancien Testament" (Paris 1957)

W. L. Moran: "The Ancient Near Eastern Background of the Love of God in Deuteronomy" (*Catholic Biblical Quarterly 25*, 1963, 77-87)

V. Warnach: "Agapé. Die Liebe als Grundmotiv der neutestamentlichen Theologie" (Düsseldorf 1951)

C. Spicq: "Agapé. Prolégomènes" (*Studia Hellenistica:* Louvain 1955)

Idem: "Agapè dans le Nouveau Testament" (Paris 1958-1960)

E. Walter: "Geloof, hoop en liefde in het Nieuwe Testament" (Bussum 1953)

K. Romaniuk: "L'amour du Père et du Fils dans la sotériologie de St. Paul" (Rome 1961)

L. Lyonett: "Paul," *Introduction à la Bible* II (Tournai 1959)

B. Allo: "Jean" *Supplément au Dictionnaire de la Bible* 21, 815

A. Feuillet: "Jean" *Introduction à la Bible* II (Tournai 1959)

T. Barosse: "Christianity, Mystery of Love" *Catholic Biblical Quarterly 20*, 1958, 137-172)